CRANE'S WEDDING BLUE BOOK

Steven L. Feinberg

A FIRESIDE BOOK
Published by Simon & Schuster
New York London Toronto Sydney Tokyo Singapore

FIRESIDE

Rockefeller Center
1230 Avenue of the Americas
New York, New York 10020

FIRESIDE and colophon are registered trademarks
of Simon & Schuster Inc.

Designed by Bonni Leon-Berman

Manufactured in the United States of America

7   9   10   8

Library of Congress Cataloging in Publication Data
Feinberg, Steven L.
Crane's wedding blue book : the styles and etiquette of invitations,
announcements, and other correspondence / Steven L. Feinberg.
p.   cm.
"A Fireside book."
Includes index.
1. Wedding etiquette.   2. Invitation cards.   I. Crane (Firm)
II. Title.
BJ2051.F45   1993
395'.4—dc20   92-37613
CIP

ISBN: 0-671-79641-0

CONTENTS

INTRODUCTION

A NOTE TO THE BRIDE

As our society evolves, so does our etiquette. The changing role of women, the unfortunate increase in the divorce rate, and the fact that men and women are marrying later in life are all contributing factors. Many of the rules of etiquette were made (and continue to be made) to deal with difficult and changing social situations. Some of the etiquette deemed proper in this book would have been unthinkable a generation ago. And, surely, a generation from now many of the guidelines presented here will seem archaic and obsolete.

When all is said and done, etiquette is based on common sense and courtesy. Your guests need certain information to get them to your wedding—the names of the hosts, what the event is, and the date, time, and place. You want, of course, to convey this information to them as graciously as possible. A courteous invitation makes all your guests feel wanted and never hurts anybody's feelings.

At Crane & Co. we receive many questions from brides concerning proper wording for their wedding invitations and other related items. *Crane's Wedding Blue Book* has been written in an attempt to answer your questions and to help make your wedding preparations go as smoothly as possible.

BEFORE THE WEDDING

ENGAGEMENT ANNOUNCEMENTS

Once you become engaged, you may want to share your excitement with others by officially announcing it. The announcement is traditionally made by your parents as soon after the engagement as possible. While there are no strict rules regarding the wording of engagement announcements, they are usually pretty straightforward.

Mr. and Mrs. Andrew Jay Forrester

announce the engagement of their daughter

Jennifer Marie

to

Mr. Nicholas Jude Strickland

February the fourteenth

Nineteen hundred and ninety-eight

Is it appropriate to send engagement announcements? Doesn't the newspaper announcement suffice?

Newspaper announcements are great but they only reach those people who subscribe to that paper. If you want to make sure that all of your friends and family members find out about your engagement, you need to send announcements—or make a lot of phone calls.

I would like to send engagement announcements but I am afraid people will think I am asking for a gift.

An engagement announcement is not a request for a gift. It is simply intended to announce an event—your engagement. Nobody receiving an announcement should feel obligated to send a gift.

INVITATIONS TO AN ENGAGEMENT PARTY

Your engagement may be celebrated with a party hosted by your parents. If your parents live out of town and it is more practical for your fiancé's parents to host a party, they may do so instead. The invitations say that the event is being held in honor of you and your fiancé, although they do not usually mention that it is in honor of your engagement. The guests will undoubtedly figure it out on their own.

The invitations are generally engraved, but for small parties fill-in invitations may be used.

Mr. and Mrs. Andrew Jay Forrester

request the pleasure of your company

at a dinner in honor of

Miss Jennifer Marie Forrester

and

Mr. Nicholas Jude Strickland

Friday, the thirtieth of March

at seven o'clock

2830 Meadowbrook Drive

Bedford, New York

Our engagement will be announced at the party. How should the invitations read?

If your engagement is being announced at an engagement party, neither your name nor your fiancé's should appear on the invitation, as that would likely give away the surprise. The invitations read as though they are not for any special event other than to enjoy the company of family and good friends.

Two of my parents' closest friends have offered to host my engagement party. How should the invitations read?

When an engagement party is hosted by friends of your parents, the invitations are issued by your parents' friends so their names appear on the first line of the invitations. Your parents' names are not mentioned.

INVITATIONS TO MEET YOU OR YOUR FIANCÉ

In lieu of an engagement party or in addition to an engagement party hosted by the other set of parents, a party to meet you or your fiancé may be in order. If, for example, your parents held an engagement party in New York and your fiancé's parents in California wanted to host a party as well, they may host a party "to meet" you. This party gives their family (your future in-laws) and friends an opportunity to get to know you before the wedding. The party is in your honor and the invitations allude to that.

To meet

Miss Jennifer Marie Forrester

Mr. and Mrs. John Peter Strickland

request the pleasure of your company

at a cocktail reception

Friday, the sixth of March

at eight o'clock

910 Oakland Avenue

San Marino, California

INVITATIONS TO A BRIDAL SHOWER

The modern bridal shower is a throwback to the days when a bride brought her dowry to the marriage. Provided by her father, the dowry made her more attractive to potential husbands and gave the newly married couple material goods and finances to help them start their new lives together. Modern bridal showers, attended by family and friends, allow today's brides and grooms to have the basic necessities to furnish their new homes.

Bridal showers are hosted by one or more friends of the bride. The invitations are usually informal. They may be engraved, but many times fill-in invitations are used.

Many bridal showers have gift themes, such as linens, kitchen, and lingerie. For older brides, the themes might include tennis, golf, garden, and travel. When a shower has a theme, the theme is mentioned in the lower right-hand corner.

Maureen McGlamery

requests the pleasure of your company

at a Bridal Shower

in honor of

Jennifer Forrester

Tuesday, the tenth of August

at seven o'clock

19 Crescent Drive

Bedford, New York

Please reply
(914) 555-1212

Kitchen

Maureen McGlamery   Pamela Mennis

Jean Shepard   Judy Romero

Kathy Connelly   Robin Abrams

invite you to a surprise Bridal Shower

in honor of

Jennifer Forrester

Tuesday, August tenth

at seven o'clock

19 Crescent Drive

Bedford, New York

Please respond
Maureen McGlamery
(914) 555-1212   Linens

I'm being married for the second time. Is it appropriate for somebody to host a shower for me?

Historically, bridal showers have been reserved for first-time brides. That, however, is a tradition that is changing. Showers are now being given for second-time brides, especially if she did not have one before her first wedding.

Can my sister host a shower for me?

Since the purpose of a shower is to receive gifts, it is inappropriate for any member of your immediate family to host one. It may appear as though they are soliciting gifts for you at your request.

INVITATIONS TO A BRIDAL TEA

In some parts of the United States, close friends of the bride host teas in her honor. The invitations mention that the tea is being given in your honor and may also state your fiancé's name by announcing that you are his "bride-elect." Invitations to bridal teas are, generally, engraved in black ink on ecru or white card stock.

Mrs. Geoffrey Harold Fenwick
requests the pleasure of your company
at a bridal tea for
Miss Jennifer Marie Forrester
Thursday, the seventh of August
at four o'clock
261 Sycamore Street
Bedford

Mrs. Geoffrey Harold Fenwick
requests the pleasure of your company
at a tea for
Miss Jennifer Marie Forrester
bride-elect of
Mr. Nicholas Jude Strickland
Thursday, the seventh of August
at four o'clock
261 Sycamore Street
Bedford

REHEARSAL DINNER INVITATIONS

Custom suggests that the groom's parents host the rehearsal dinner and, therefore, issue its invitations. The rehearsal dinner takes place on the night before the wedding and is given as a courtesy to the bride's family. The rehearsal dinner invitations are usually worded formally, but many times just first names are used. This less formal style can be a way to let guests know how you, your fiancé, and your fiancé's parents wish to be addressed.

Just as the rehearsal dinner should not compete with or upstage the wedding, the invitations to the rehearsal dinner should complement the wedding invitations, although they should not match them. For example, a rehearsal dinner invitation on a flat white card engraved in navy blue ink nicely complements a formal wedding invitation.

Mr. and Mrs. John Peter Strickland

request the pleasure of your company

at a rehearsal dinner

in honour of

Miss Jennifer Marie Forrester

and

Mr. Nicholas Jude Strickland

Friday, the twenty-second of August

at half after seven o'clock

Tappan Hill

Tarrytown, New York

Nellie and John Strickland

request the pleasure of your company

at a rehearsal dinner for

Jennifer and Nick

Friday, August twenty-second

at seven-thirty

Tappan Hill

Tarrytown, New York

Who is invited to the rehearsal dinner?

Traditionally, the rehearsal dinner was held for just the wedding party in order to get them fed after the rehearsal—and to give the bride's mother one less thing to be responsible for. While many rehearsal dinners are still reserved for the wedding party, others have expanded to include the wedding party, their spouses or dates, and out-of-town guests.

When are rehearsal dinner invitations sent?

The invitations are sent two weeks before the wedding.

Very few people are being invited to our rehearsal dinner. Do we need engraved invitations?

For small dinners, it is appropriate for the groom's parents to use their "Mr. and Mrs." informals or a fill-in invitation. (Informals are small fold-over notes that are always ecru or white and engraved in black ink with the name(s) centered on the front.) If they choose to use their informals, they may either write the information on the front of the informal or write a short note inviting their guests on the inside.

FACE:

Dinner   *7:30*   *August 22nd*

Mr. and Mrs. John Peter Strickland

Tappan Hill

INSIDE:

Dear Kelly and Steven,

John and I would like you to join us for dinner after the rehearsal at Tappan Hill in Tarrytown.
We look forward to seeing you.

Love,
Nellie

SAVE-THE-DATE CARDS

Weekends during the holiday and summer seasons tend to be busy times for some people. If you are planning your wedding for one of these seasons, you may wish to send save-the-date cards. These cards, sent at least three months before the wedding, advise family and friends of your wedding plans and allow them to take your wedding date into consideration when making their own plans. Save-the-date cards are also sent when a number of overseas guests are invited and when a wedding is held in a resort area, since some guests might like to plan a vacation around your wedding.

Save-the-date cards are small, heavy ecru or white cards and are mailed in an envelope. They should match the wedding invitations.

Please save the date of
Saturday, the twenty-third of August
for the wedding of
Miss Jennifer Marie Forrester
to
Mr. Nicholas Jude Strickland

Mr. and Mrs. Andrew Jay Forrester

Invitation to follow

To whom are save-the-date cards sent?

They may be sent to all guests but it is especially important for out-of-town guests to receive them as they will have to make travel arrangements. However, if they are sent only to your out-of-town guests and your out-of-town guests speak to your in-town guests, your in-town guests might feel slighted, thinking that they are not going to be invited to your wedding.

WEDDING
INVITATIONS
AND
ANNOUNCEMENTS

SELECTING YOUR WEDDING INVITATION

Wedding invitations set the tone for the wedding; they are the first exposure most people will have to your wedding, and will create your guests' first impressions. Not only do your invitations tell them where and when your wedding is being held, they subtly tell them how formal it is, how they should dress, and may even influence the types of gifts they send.

When you select your wedding invitations, keep in mind what kind of wedding you are having. Your invitations and your wedding should complement one another. While formal invitations are appropriate for, among other things, a traditional church wedding, something less formal and more colorful may be more suitable for a wedding held at sunset on a beach.

Wedding invitations should be ordered at least three months before your wedding. This should leave you enough time for engraving, addressing, and mailing. (Wedding invitations should be mailed four to six weeks before the wedding.) Of course, it is best to order them as soon as you have all the necessary information.

Where should I go to purchase my wedding invitations?

There are many places that sell wedding invitations including stationery stores, jewelers, engravers, department stores, and specialty stores. When selecting a stationer, you should look for one who has expertise in selling wedding invitations and whom you feel comfortable working with. Your stationer should be able to answer or find the answers to any questions that you might have.

What kind of paper should I use?

This is actually a three-part question, as you need to choose the material from which the paper is made, the color, and the type of stationery.

Wedding papers are made from either cotton or wood. The first true papers were made from cotton almost two thousand years ago. Wood-pulp papers came into being in the 1800s during the industrial revolution. They supplanted cotton-fiber papers for many uses because of their lower cost and the seemingly endless supply of trees.

The finest paper, though, is made from cotton. Before you order your invitations, run your fingers across the paper. Invitations made from cotton will have a soft, rich feel to them. You'll be able to recognize the luxury and the quality inherent in cotton-fiber paper.

There are other advantages to using cotton-fiber papers. In addition to the superior quality, papers made from 100 percent cotton are environmentally friendly. Cotton is a renewable resource. A new cotton crop is harvested every year, whereas it takes many years to replace the trees used to make wood-pulp papers. And unlike papers made from ordinary wood pulp, papers made from cotton do not decompose. Your wedding invitations will look as beautiful on your Golden Wedding Anniversary as they did on the day you sent them.

Formal wedding invitations can be engraved on either ecru or white stationery. Ecru is the color you may know as buff, cream, ivory, or eggshell. It is the off-white color that we typically associate with wedding invitations. The color that you choose is a matter of personal preference. Ecru is the more popular of the two in the Americas while white is the color of choice in Europe.

Formal wedding invitations have a fold on the left-hand side and open like a book. This type of stationery is called a letter sheet. They may be either plain or paneled. Paneled invitations have a blind embossed frame. The decision on which one to choose is usually determined by the lettering style that you select. Script styles tend to look better with no panel around them while most other styles tend to look best on paneled invitations. If you choose to do a script lettering style within a panel, you should ask to see a proof so you can see what the invitation will look like before it goes to press. While some script lettering styles can look beautiful on paneled invitations, they are condensed to fit the panel, so they may not look the way you expect them to. A proof eliminates surprises and is a wise investment.

What size should my invitations be?

Wedding invitations are available in three different sizes: 6⅜ by 8⅞ inches, 5½ by 7½ inches, and 4½ by 6¼ inches. Each of these letter sheets fits in a set of matching envelopes.

The two larger sizes are also available with a second fold across the middle of the sheet. The sheets fold a second time from top to bottom. The fold runs beneath the "to" line and does not cut across any of the engraving. These invitations are the most traditional. If you look at your parents' or grandparents' wedding invitations, you will more than likely find that they were done with a second fold.

These traditional invitations date back to earlier times when most formal social events were held in cities and towns. The residents had relatively small mailboxes so instead of having the postman stuff large invitations into small mailboxes, engravers folded the invitations neatly into smaller envelopes.

There must be hundreds of different lettering styles. How do I go about choosing one?

Selecting a lettering style can be a tiresome and confusing task. Style charts present just one line of each particular style surrounded by a myriad of other styles and, therefore, do not give you a very good idea of how the whole invitation will look. The best way to choose a lettering style is to skip the style charts and look at the sample invitations. This allows you to see what your invitations will look like in each lettering style. Since traditional invitations all follow the same format, your invitations will look pretty much like the sample in the book.

The lettering style that you do choose should reflect the formality of your wedding and your personal taste. Classic lettering styles, such as Royal Script or Shaded Antique Roman, are the most popular and are always in good taste.

WEDDING TYPE STYLES

Mr. and Mrs. Andrew Jay Forrester

ROYAL SCRIPT

Mr. and Mrs. Andrew Jay Forrester

SHADED ANTIQUE ROMAN

M$^{r.}$ and M$^{rs.}$ Andrew Jay Forrester

LONDON SCRIPT

Mr. and Mrs. Andrew Jay Forrester

ST. JAMES

Mr. and Mrs. Andrew Jay Forrester

STATESMAN

Mr. and Mrs. Andrew Jay Forrester

FLORIDIAN

Mr. and Mrs. Andrew Jay Forrester

CAVALIER SCRIPT

Mr. and Mrs. Andrew Jay Forrester

DORIC TEXT

Mr. and Mrs. Andrew Jay Forrester

FLEMISH SCRIPT

Mr. and Mrs. Andrew Jay Forrester

ROOK SCRIPT

What color ink should I use?

Formal wedding invitations are engraved in black ink. However, exceptionally bold lettering styles on white invitations can look too heavy and busy when engraved in black ink. In such cases, it is permissible to use dark gray ink. Other colors, however, are not appropriate for traditional invitations, although they may be used on less formal ones.

What is engraving?

Engraving is one of the oldest and most beautiful processes for reproducing images on paper. It was developed during the 1700s and was initially used to reproduce the documents and announcements that were at that time copied by hand. The appeal of engraving was in the exquisite detail created by its three-dimensional impression.

Engravers were talented craftsmen who carried their trade from the Old World to the Americas. Their craft was not only used to produce stationery and announcements but also currency papers, such as stocks, bonds, and dollar bills. Two of the United States' most famous engravers were Paul Revere and Benjamin Franklin.

The most elegant invitations are still engraved. The invitation copy is etched in reverse into a copper plate. Ink is deposited into the resulting cavity. The engraving press then forces the paper into the cavity, creating a raised impression. The paper is literally raised with the ink adhering to its raised surface. The fact that the paper itself is raised is what distinguishes engraving from printing and thermography.

How can I tell if an invitation is engraved?

The easiest way is to turn it over and look at the back. If there is an indentation, it is engraved.

The indentation is caused by the pressure the engraving press exerts on the paper when it forces the paper into the cavity of the die. None of the other processes produce an indentation. When you look at the front of the invitation, you will notice its "bruise." The invitation will have a gentle wave or ripple to it, giving it a look of distinction. Run your fingers across it. You will feel the softness of the cotton paper interrupted by the sharp, crisp lines that can only be created by engraving.

What is thermography?

Thermography is sometimes called "raised printing," although the printing is not raised at all. Unlike engraving where the paper is actually raised, the raise in thermography is created by a resinous powder that is melted over the flat-printed ink. Thermography is less expensive than engraving and can give your invitations a look similar to but not quite as nice as engraving.

What is blind embossing?

Blind embossing (or just "embossing") is a process similar to engraving. As with engraving, a raised impression is created from a copper plate. Unlike engraving, no ink is used. Blind embossing is commonly used for a family coat of arms, the return address on the outside envelopes, and monogrammed thank-you notes. Dies made for blind embossing can be used again to blind emboss or to engrave in a metallic color. They cannot, however, be engraved in other ink colors.

When should my wedding invitations be mailed?

Wedding invitations should be mailed four to six weeks before the wedding. For summer and holiday weddings, many brides mail their invitations eight weeks before the wedding since people are more likely to be traveling at those times.

How much postage will my wedding invitations require?

The invitation's size, the number of enclosure cards, and even the humidity affect the postage. To determine the correct postage, you should have your invitations (including the stamp on the reply envelope) weighed at the post office from which they will be sent.

How much money should I expect to spend?

Costs will vary as they are determined by the quality of the invitation, the number of enclosures, and the quantity ordered. When selecting your invitations, it is important to remember that even though the invitations set the tone for the entire wedding, they comprise, on average, only about 2 percent of the total cost of the wedding. No matter how much money you save by purchasing inexpensive invitations, it will be a tiny amount in relation to the overall cost of your wedding.

COMPOSING YOUR WEDDING INVITATION

The traditional wedding invitation has changed little over the years. Its essential purpose is to invite your guests and to tell them where and when your wedding is being held. Most other information is superfluous. It is this simplicity, coupled with fine paper and distinctive engraving, that make formal wedding invitations so elegant.

There are a number of basic points of etiquette that should be followed when wording a traditional wedding invitation. The following section covers the correct wording line by line.

COAT OF ARMS

Some of the most distinctive wedding invitations feature a coat of arms. If your family has one, it may be used on your wedding invitations. When used, the coat of arms is always blind embossed at the top of the invitations. It is never proper to engrave it in a color on wedding invitations.

Because it is blind embossed, an engraving die is needed. If your family does not already have a die, one needs to be made. That will take additional time so you will need to order your invitations early.

What is a coat of arms?
Originally, a coat of arms was the armor a knight wore into battle. To identify him as friend or foe, an insignia was emblazed on the front. This insignia was transformed into what we now think of as a coat of arms: a small symbol, unique to each family that has one.

A full coat of arms is made up of the crest, the helmet, the shield, and the motto. Mantling may also be added. The coat of arms "belongs" to the men in the family and may be used on invitations issued by a man or by a man and his wife. Since, historically, women did not go into battle, they do not use a full coat of arms when issuing invitations themselves. Instead, women use their husband's crests or another device called a lozenge, which is a diamond-shaped symbol in which her family's coat of arms is combined with her husband's.

Is our coat of arms blind embossed on our reception cards as well?
The use of a coat of arms is reserved for the invitation. It is not properly used on enclosure cards.

My fiancé and I are issuing our own wedding invitations. Whose coat of arms do we use?
A coat of arms is not used when the bride and groom issue their own wedding invitations.

My fiancé's parents are issuing our wedding invitations. Is it proper to use their coat of arms?
Your fiancé's family is entitled to use their coat of arms whenever they issue invitations.

Mr. and Mrs. Andrew Jay Forrester

INVITATIONAL LINE

request the honour of your presence

REQUEST LINES

at the marriage of their daughter

Jennifer Marie

BRIDE'S NAME

to

JOINING WORD

Mr. Nicholas Jude Strickland

GROOM'S NAME

Saturday, the twenty-third of August

DATE LINE

One thousand, nine hundred and ninety-seven

YEAR LINE

at six o'clock

TIME LINE

Church of Christ

LOCATION

1223 Roaring Brook Road

ADDRESS

Bedford, New York

CITY AND STATE

INVITATIONAL LINE

Wedding invitations are properly issued by the parents of the bride. This tradition and the tradition of the bride's father giving away the bride have their origins in the days when the bride's father made the marriage arrangements for his daughter by negotiating the size of her dowry. Today, the tradition continues with the bride's family customarily hosting the wedding. Therefore, the names of the bride's parents appear on the first line of the wedding invitations.

Mr. and Mrs. Andrew Jay Forrester

request the honour of your presence

at the marriage of their daughter

Jennifer Marie

etc.

My father is a medical doctor. Does he use his title?

Medical doctors do use their professional titles. "Doctor" should be written out. However, it may be abbreviated to "Dr." if your father's name is exceptionally long.

My mother is a medical doctor but my father is not. How is that worded?

Traditionally, your mother would use her social title—"Mrs."—on your wedding invitations, so your parents names should read, "Mr. and Mrs. Andrew Jay Forrester." However, times are changing. As more and more women have become doctors, they have felt it unfair that male doctors can properly use their professional titles while they are relegated to "Mrs." While it is still most proper for women doctors to use their social titles, they may also, quite properly, use their professional titles instead.

If your mother chooses to use her professional title, her name, preceded by her title, appears on the first line. Your father's name and title, preceded by "and," appears on the second line. The use of "and" indicates that they are married. Were you not to use "and" it would appear as though your parents were divorced.

Doctor Mary Chance Forrester

and Mr. Andrew Jay Forrester

request the honour of your presence

at the marriage of their daughter

Jennifer Marie

etc.

Both of my parents are medical doctors. How do their names read?
Your parents' names most properly would read, "Doctor and Mrs. Andrew Jay Forrester" but may read, "The Doctors Forrester" or "Doctor Mary Chance Forrester / and Doctor Andrew Jay Forrester" instead.

My mother kept her maiden name. How should my parents' names read?
One alternative is to discuss with your parents the possibility of their using "Mr. and Mrs. Andrew Jay Forrester" for purposes of the wedding invitation. Another alternative is to engrave your mother's name on the first line of the invitation and your father's name, preceded by "and" on line two. No titles are used in this format.

Mary Ellen Chance
and Andrew Jay Forrester
request the honour of your presence
at the marriage of their daughter
Jennifer Marie
to
Nicholas Jude Strickland
etc.

My father has a Ph.D. Does he use "Doctor" on my wedding invitations?

Ph.D. is an academic title that is used only in academic settings. The use of "Doctor" on wedding invitations is reserved for medical doctors and ministers with advanced degrees.

My father is a minister. How should my parents' names read?

The invitational line should read, "The Reverend and Mrs. Andrew Jay Forrester." A minister who holds a doctorate uses "The Reverend Doctor Andrew Jay Forrester." Neither "Reverend" nor "Doctor" should be abbreviated. If the invitational line becomes too long, it may be split to read, "The Reverend Doctor / and Mrs. Andrew Jay Forrester."

My mother is a minister but my father is not. How do their names read?

Women traditionally use their social titles on social invitations so your parents' names should read, "Mr. and Mrs. Andrew Jay Forrester." If your mother chooses to use her theological title, the first line would read, "The Reverend Mary Chance Forrester." Your father's name would be given on the second line which would read, "and Mr. Andrew Jay Forrester."

My father is a judge. Does he use "The Honorable?"

"The Honorable" is always used when addressing a judge. However, when a judge issues an invitation, he does not use "The Honorable" since it would be presumptuous for him to bestow that title upon himself. He may use "Judge" as his title.

My mother is a judge but my father is not. How should their names read?

Your mother most properly uses her social title, which is "Mrs." Should she wish to use her professional title, her name would appear on the first line of the invitation preceded by "Judge." The second would read, "and Mr. Andrew Jay Forrester." The use of "and" indicates that they are married to each other.

My fiancé and I are paying for our wedding. How is that indicated?

There is no proper way to indicate that you and your fiancé are paying for your wedding. Your guests, however, will probably assume that you and your fiancé are paying for your wedding if you issue the invitations yourselves. You may also have your parents issue the invitations to the ceremony while you and your fiancé issue the invitation to the reception. The reception card would have your name and title on the first line and your fiancé's name and title on the second line. The rest of the reception card would read, "request the pleasure of your company / at the marriage reception / immediately following the ceremony" followed by the name of the facility at which the reception will be held.

My father dislikes his middle name. Is it proper to use his middle initial?

Formal wedding invitations require the use of full names. Initials should not be used. If your father insists on not using his middle name, it is better to omit it entirely than to use an initial.

My father's middle name is just an initial. Is it proper to use his initial?

It is proper to use just his initial as long as the initial is his full middle name.

DIVORCED PARENTS

Some of the most difficult situations in wording wedding invitations occur when the parents of the bride are divorced. There are simple and straightforward rules to handle these situations but sometimes emotions take control of circumstances and render these rules inadequate. You may find yourself unable to follow the prescribed rules of etiquette to a tee for fear of offending a family member or creating additional, unnecessary tensions. If you find yourself in this situation, you may choose to go a different route and find wording that is both appropriate and innocuous. Etiquette is intended as a guide to good taste and to facilitate good relationships and the comfort of everyone. Therefore, in such an instance it is entirely appropriate for you to stray from the accepted rules.

The proper way to word an invitation when the bride's parents are divorced is to list the names of the bride's parents at the top of the invitation. Her mother's name is on the first line and her father's name is on the line beneath it. The lines are not separated by "and."

If the bride's mother has not remarried, she uses "Mrs." followed by her first name, maiden name, and married name. The old etiquette called for using just her maiden name and her last name, preceded by "Mrs." The change evolved over the years as it was increasingly felt that the old usage was too impersonal.

When the bride's mother is divorced from the bride's father and has remarried, she uses "Mrs." followed by her husband's full name.

My parents are divorced and my father has remarried. Where does his wife's name appear?

Traditionally, you are "given away" by your parents. Therefore, it is generally only the names of your natural parents that properly appear on your wedding invitations, although, of course, there are exceptions. One obvious exception involves a bride who was adopted, in which case the names of the parents who raised her appear. Another exception to the rule can occur when the bride's mother was widowed and remarried when the bride was at a relatively young age. Although her stepfather never adopted her, he did help raise her and, in effect, acted as her father. In such a case, it is appropriate for his name to appear on the invitations.

I'm afraid that if I don't include the name of my father's wife on my invitations, it might hurt her feelings.

Etiquette should never be adhered to at the cost of damaging a relationship. Its purpose is to build relationships, not to harm them. There are ways to handle any situation that will accommodate everybody involved.

Since it is not proper for the name of your father's wife to appear on the invitations, a nice compromise might be to word the invitations properly with just your parents' names on them while including the name of your father's wife on the reception cards. This way, she is listed with your parents as one of the hosts of the reception. By doing this, she is given a place of honor on the reception cards while the invitations are still worded properly.

If you choose to do this, your mother's name would be on the first line of the reception card. The second line would have the names of your father and his wife. The remainder of the card reads, "request the pleasure of your company / at the marriage reception" followed by the date, time, and place.

My parents are divorced and my father is paying for the wedding. How is that indicated?

Wedding invitations are worded the way they are to reflect the tradition of the bride's family graciously giving away the bride while inviting family and friends to join them for this happy occasion. As with the ceremony itself, the center of attention is the bride and groom. (That's why their names are spread out in the center of the invitation.) Therefore, there is no place to indicate who is paying the bills. To do so would be to draw attention away from the bride and groom.

If, after this explanation, you still feel a need to let people know that your father is picking up the tab, you may do so on the reception cards. The reception cards serve as invitations to the reception. By listing your father as host of the reception, you will be indicating to your guests that he is paying for it. This way, you have properly worded wedding invitations and reception cards that convey to your guests the fact that your father is funding the wedding.

Instead of reading, "Reception / immediately following the ceremony," your reception cards would read, "Mr. Andrew Jay Forrester / requests the pleasure of your company / at the marriage reception" followed by the date, time, and place.

My mother is divorced and has resumed using her maiden name. What title should she use?

Your mother's name should appear on the invitations without a title. When this is done, all other titles should be omitted so that the invitation retains a uniform appearance.

Why isn't "and" used between the names of divorced parents?

By using "and" between the names of divorced parents, you create an additional line and a competing center of attention. With the extra line your eye is drawn to both the top of the invitation and the center. It should be drawn directly to the center where the names of the bride and groom appear.

SEPARATED PARENTS

When the bride's parents are legally separated, they may issue their daughter's wedding invitations together. Their names may appear on separate lines with the name of the bride's mother on the first line and the bride's father's name on the second line. The word "and" is not used to join their names. The bride's mother properly uses her married name, which is "Mrs.," followed by her husband's name. If she does not want to use "Mrs.," she can use her first, maiden, and last names without a title. This wording, however, is not proper and is, therefore, less formal. It also requires the dropping of all other titles on the invitation in order to keep the rest of the invitation uniform.

The bride's parents may also, when legally separated but not divorced, issue their daughter's wedding invitations together as "Mr. and Mrs."

WIDOWED PARENTS

When one of the bride's parents is deceased, her wedding invitations are issued by her surviving parent. His or her name appears alone on the invitational line. In most cases, stepparents' names are not used.

A widow retains the use of her husband's name. If she has not remarried, she continues to be known as "Mrs. Andrew Jay Forrester." If she has remarried, she uses "Mrs." followed by her present husband's name. In this case, since the bride's surname is different from her mother's surname, the bride's full name appears on the fourth line of the invitation. The bride's name is not preceded by "Miss."

Mrs. John Michael Davies

requests the honour of your presence

at the marriage of her daughter

Jennifer Marie Forrester

etc.

Two exceptions to the "no stepparents" rule occur when the bride's mother or father remarried and the bride's stepparent helped raise the bride from a young age, and when the bride feels especially close to her stepparent. In these situations, the name of the bride's stepparent may properly appear. When this is done, the third line of the invitation reads either, "at the marriage of her (his) daughter" or "at the marriage of Mrs. Davies' daughter." This suggests to your guests that, in this case, your mother is your natural parent. The use of "Mrs. Davies' daughter" is an older form that has been gradually disappearing from use. The vast majority of brides nowadays use "her daughter."

Mr. and Mrs. John Michael Davies

request the honour of your presence

at the marriage of her daughter

Jennifer Marie Forrester

etc.

When is it appropriate to use "senior"?
A man who is a "junior" usually stops using "junior" upon his father's death. If he is married, his widowed mother uses "senior" to distinguish herself from her daughter-in-law. "Senior" should be spelled out using a lowercase *s*. It may be abbreviated to "Sr." when used with an especially long name.

My mother is a widow who has not remarried. She prefers the use of her first name. Can her name read, "Mrs. Mary Chance Forrester?"
A widow who has not remarried should use her deceased husband's name, preceded by "Mrs." (A divorced woman uses "Mrs." followed by her first, maiden, and married names.) If your mother would rather use her first name, she should do so without her title. Using names without titles on an invitation, however, is generally considered incorrect and makes the invitation less formal than it otherwise would be. If your mother's title is omitted, all other titles should be left off the invitation as well. This is done to keep the wording of the invitation consistent.

My father passed away last year and I would like to include his name on my wedding invitations. How is that done?
While wishing to include a deceased parent's name on a wedding invitation is a lovely sentiment, it is not proper to do so (except in Latin

America). The essential purpose of a wedding invitation is to invite your guests to your wedding and to tell them where and when it is taking place. It lists the host or hosts of the event, what the event is (your wedding), and the date, time, and place. The only logical place to list your father's name is on an invitational line. This, however, is improper as he would be listed as one of the hosts of your wedding. Since he is deceased, he cannot be a host.

Your father's name is, of course, mentioned in your newspaper announcement and may also be mentioned in the wedding program and during a prayer said during the service. Your wedding is a joyous occasion. Reminding your guests of your father's death by adding "and the late Mr. Andrew Jay Forrester" introduces an element of sadness to an otherwise joyous occasion.

The Hispanic tradition, on the other hand, does include the name of a deceased parent. If the deceased parent is the bride's father, her mother's name appears alone on the first line and her father's name, followed by a small cross if Christian or a Star of David if Jewish, appears on line two. One note of caution: Your guests may not be familiar with this custom and may not understand the meaning of it.

Mrs. John Carlos Aponte

Mr. John Carlos Aponte †

request the honour of your presence

at the marriage of their daughter

Jennifer Marie

etc.

INVITATIONS ISSUED BY THE BRIDE
AND GROOM

Although it is most proper for the parents of the bride to issue their daughter's wedding invitations, there may be times when the bride and groom choose to issue the invitations themselves. This course of action is often taken when the bride's parents are deceased. Many brides and grooms issue their own invitations when they are an older couple or when the bride is marrying for the second time.

There are two proper formats for self-invitations. The more formal of the two contains no invitational line. The less formal format lists both the bride and groom as hosts.

The honour of your presence

is requested at the marriage of

Miss Jennifer Marie Forrester

to

Mr. Nicholas Jude Strickland

etc.

Miss Jennifer Marie Forrester

and

Mr. Nicholas Jude Strickland

request the honour of your presence

at their marriage

etc.

Although my fiancé and I are not medical doctors now, we will be before our wedding. Is it proper for us to use "Doctor" on our invitations?

Since you will be medical doctors on the day you are married, it is proper for you to use your new titles.

My fiancé and I are paying for our wedding. How is that indicated?

As long as they are alive, your parents properly issue your wedding invitations, regardless of who is paying. Most people, however, will assume that the two of you are paying for your wedding if your parents' names are not mentioned.

SECOND MARRIAGES

According to many studies, about half of all Americans will divorce and remarry. Subsequently, a growing number of wedding invitations issued today involve a bride or groom marrying for a second time. When either the bride or both the bride and the groom are marrying for the second time, the wedding invitations are issued by the bride and groom themselves. A bride who is being married for the first time to a groom who is marrying for the second time, typically, has her invitations issued by her parents. In other words, it is the bride's status that determines the wording of the invitation. The groom's previous marital status does not affect the invitations.

Traditionally, a divorced bride marrying for the second time used her first name, maiden name, and married name preceded by "Mrs." on her wedding invitations. Through the years, this has changed as the great majority of brides have felt that the inclusion of "Mrs." on their wedding invitations was unnecessary and inappropriate. Today, it is entirely appropriate not to use "Mrs." and almost every bride chooses to omit it.

Second-time brides who are divorced, therefore, use just their first, middle, and last names on their invitations. No title is used. Whenever the bride's title is omitted, the groom's title is also omitted. This keeps the wording of the invitations consistent.

Widows marrying again properly use "Mrs." followed by their deceased husband's name. A young widow, however, may have her parents issue her invitations, even if they issued the invitations to her first wedding. A young widow uses her first, maiden, and married names. No title is used.

The most formal wording for a second marriage omits the invitational line. A less formal, but still correct wording places the bride and groom's names at the top of the invitation.

DIVORCED BRIDE:

The honour of your presence

is requested at the marriage of

Jennifer Forrester O'Neal

to

Nicholas Jude Strickland

etc.

Jennifer Marie Forrester

and

Nicholas Jude Strickland

request the honour of your presence

at their marriage

etc.

WIDOWED BRIDE:

The honour of your presence

is requested at the marriage of

Mrs. James Richard Celestino

to

Mr. Nicholas Jude Strickland

etc.

My parents sent traditional invitations for my first wedding. Is it proper for me to send traditional invitations for my second wedding?

Wedding invitations set the tone for the wedding, regardless of whether it is a first, second, or third wedding. If your wedding is going to be a traditional one, you should send traditional invitations.

Many second weddings, however, are less formal. The invitations to these weddings may be informal. Instead of an ecru letter sheet, a card bordered in a bright color or decorative design may be used. The invitation may be engraved or printed in ink to match the border. As a finishing touch, the envelopes can be lined in a matching color or pattern.

Some etiquette books claim that it is not proper to have invitations to a second wedding engraved. Is this true?

The quality inherent to engraving exists whether you are marrying for the first or second time. There is no reason why the invitations to your second wedding cannot properly be as beautifully engraved as those to your first wedding. If you appreciate the quality of engraving, then by all means have them engraved.

I am marrying for the third time. How should my name read?

Your first name, maiden name, and your second husband's last name are used. Your first husband's name is omitted entirely.

I am divorced and getting remarried. May I use "Ms." instead of "Mrs."?

"Ms." is never properly used on wedding invitations or on most other forms of social stationery. The use of "Ms." is reserved for business correspondence and, under certain circumstances, the addressing of wedding invitation envelopes. If you like, you may omit "Mrs." and use just your first, maiden, and married names. If you do that, your fiancé's title is omitted as well.

I am a doctor. Is it proper for me to use my title?

If you are a medical doctor, you may use your title on your wedding invitations. Your title precedes your name and no advanced degrees appear after it. "Doctor" should be spelled out, not abbreviated. Ph.D.'s do not properly use their academic title.

My first wedding was an elopement. This time around I am going to have a traditional wedding hosted by my parents. How should my invitations read?

Your wedding invitations read as if this were your first wedding, except for your name. Instead of just your given names, your first, maiden, and married names are used.

My first marriage was annulled. How should my wedding invitations read?

An annulment makes a marriage null and void. Therefore, you are entitled to use your maiden name. On invitations issued by your parents, your full maiden name is used, not just your given names. Your maiden name, preceded by "Miss," is used on invitations issued by you and your fiancé. Your titles may also be left off invitations that you and your fiancé issue.

We are both marrying for the second time and have no need for any more gifts. How can we let our guests know that their gifts are not necessary?

While many couples do not feel that gifts are necessary, many guests do. Asking them to not give you gifts deprives them of an opportunity to share their love with you. (It may also seem presumptuous.) Besides, the types of gifts that are given to older couples are different from those given to young brides. You may find yourselves as pleased with your presents as your guests are with giving them.

We would like our guests to donate the money they would otherwise have spent on gifts to our favorite charity. How is that indicated?

Unfortunately, there is no tactful way of doing that. While enclosing a card reading, "In lieu of gifts we ask that you send a donation to the Special Olympics" may seem to you to be an innocent enough request, it may be seen by others as presumptuous.

It is never proper to let your guests know that you expect anything from them—except the pleasure of their company.

REQUEST LINES

The request lines invite your guests to your wedding. The wording varies according to where the wedding is being held. The correct wording for a wedding held in a church, temple, synagogue, or any house of worship is, "request the honour of your presence." The word "honour" is used to show deference to God whenever a wedding is held in a house of worship. For weddings held in any location other than a house of worship, "request the pleasure of your company" is used.

Which is more formal: "request the honour of your presence" or "request the pleasure of your company"?
Both phrases are equally formal. They are just used under different circumstances.

What is the correct spelling of "honor"?
Both "honour" and "honor" are correct. It is a matter of personal preference, although the vast majority of brides prefer the English spelling, "honour."

My wedding is being held at home and is a religious ceremony. May I use "request the honour of your presence"?
The use of "request the honour of your presence" is reserved for weddings held on sanctified ground, so it is not properly used for a wedding held at home.

BRIDE'S NAME

The bride's given names are used on invitations issued by her parents. Neither her title nor her last name is used since it is assumed that she has never married and has the same last name as her parents. If her last name is different from her parents' last name, she includes her last name on her invitations.

I am a medical doctor. May I use "Doctor"?
On wedding invitations a woman traditionally uses her social title, which is either "Miss" or "Mrs." Since "Doctor" is a professional title, it would not properly appear with your name on wedding invitations. How-

ever, many brides understandably feel that this rule is unfair and proceed to break it. If you choose to go that route, you would use "Doctor" followed by your first, middle, and last names.

I am an attorney. May I use "esquire"?

"Esquire" is an English title that is not generally recognized in the United States (although some lawyers do use it to indicate that they are practicing attorneys). In England the title means "gentleman," so it is obviously inappropriate for a bride to use it.

I was adopted. Is that mentioned on my wedding invitations?

No. The parents who raised you issue your invitations and your adoption is not mentioned.

Why are the names of the bride and groom larger than the rest of the copy?

If you look closely at a wedding invitation, you will notice that all proper names (the bride, groom, bride's parents, and the church) are highlighted since these are the most important lines. The names of the bride and groom stand out even more because of the very short line ("to" or "and") that separates them.

JOINING WORD

The joining word is the word that joins the names of the bride and groom. The preposition "to" is used on invitations to the wedding ceremony as the bride is traditionally married to the groom. The conjunction "and" is used on invitations to the reception since the reception is given in honor of the bride and groom. "And" is also used on Jewish wedding invitations and on invitations issued by the bride and groom.

GROOM'S NAME

The groom always uses his full name, preceded by his title. There are no abbreviations, except for "Mr." All other titles, such as "Doctor" and "The Reverend" should be written out, although "Doctor" may be abbreviated when used with a long name. If "Doctor" is used more than once on an invitation, its use should be consistent. If it is necessary to abbreviate it with one of the names. It should be abbreviated with all names.

Initials are never properly used on formal wedding invitations. Men who dislike their middle names and use their middle initials instead should be discouraged from doing so. If your fiancé refuses to use his middle name, it is better to omit his middle name entirely than to use just his initial.

Can "junior" be abbreviated or must it be spelled out?

Properly, "junior" is written out. Abbreviating "junior" to "Jr." is less formal but still acceptable. When written out, a lowercase *j* is used. When abbreviated, the *J* is capitalized. The abbreviation is commonly used when the groom has an exceptionally long name. A comma always precedes "junior," whether written out or abbreviated.

My fiancé is a "junior." His father, however, has passed way. Does my fiancé continue to use "junior"?

Since your fiancé and his father shared the same last name, your fiancé used "junior" to distinguish himself from his father. Now that his father has passed away, he no longer needs to use "junior" and may drop it from his name. Of course, if either your fiancé or his father was a well-known public or private figure, your fiancé would continue to use "junior" to avoid any confusion.

When are the "II" and the "III" properly used?

Although it may seem as though "junior" and the "II" can be used interchangeably, they are actually different designations. "Junior" is used by a man whose father has the same name that he has, whereas the "II" is used by a man who has the same name as an older relative (usually a grandfather) other than his father.

The "III" is used by the namesake of a man using "junior" or "II."

When used on an invitation, a comma usually precedes the "II" or "III." Some men prefer to omit the comma. Either way is correct.

My fiancé is a doctor. Does his title appear on our invitations?

Medical doctors properly use their professional titles on wedding invitations, whereas Ph.D.'s do not.

Medical degrees, such as M.D. or D.D.S., are never mentioned. They are professional designations that do not belong on a social invitation.

Their use should be reserved for business cards and professional letterheads.

My fiancé is a lawyer. May he use "esquire"?

While some lawyers have adopted "esquire" as a title to designate their status as attorneys, "esquire" is not recognized as a proper title for social invitations in the United States. In England, the title means "gentleman" and is used to honor a man when addressing him. For a man to bestow that designation upon himself is presumptuous and not in good taste.

My fiancé is known by his nickname. Since none of our friends know his real name, would it be appropriate to put his nickname in parentheses?

Nicknames are never properly used on traditional wedding invitations. The names on your fiancé's birth certificate should be used.

DATE LINE

The day of the week and the date are written out in full. Abbreviations and numerals are not used. The day of the week is first, followed by the date of the month and the month itself. The day of the week may be preceded by "on." The use of "on," however, is unnecessary and may make the line too long.

You may include the time of day, as in, "Saturday evening." That is not usually necessary, however, as most people are able to determine whether your invitation is for the morning or evening without specifically being told. For example, an invitation reading, "at six o'clock" is obviously meant for six o'clock in the evening. If that invitation were meant for six o'clock in the morning, it would then be necessary to include "Saturday morning" since that would be unusual.

Invitations for weddings held at eight, nine, or ten o'clock should designate morning or evening since weddings are held at those times during both mornings and evenings. Many Roman Catholic weddings, for example, are held at those times in the morning since most Nuptial Masses are held before noon, while some Jewish weddings are held at those times on Saturday evenings so that guests and participants can wait until after sundown to travel on the Sabbath.

The time of day can be noted on the time line instead.

At what times do "afternoon" and "evening" begin?
Afternoon begins at twelve o'clock. Evening starts at six o'clock.

YEAR LINE

Since wedding invitations are sent four to six weeks before the wedding, it is not necessary to include the year. Your guests will assume that the invitation is for the next August twenty-third and not for some other August twenty-third in the distant future.

Although it is not necessary to include the year, it is not improper to do so. Your invitations will, undoubtedly, be saved by family and friends as a remembrance and may even be passed down to your children, grandchildren, and great-grandchildren. Including the year on your invitations will help your descendants remember your wedding day.

There are a couple of cautions, though, about including the year.

First, many lettering styles, especially some of the script lettering styles, look better with fewer lines of copy. Additional lines might make your invitation look too cluttered.

Second, the year line is a long, heavy line that follows two other heavy lines (the groom's name and the date). This creates a lot of weight in that part of the invitation, which can draw your eye there instead of to the names of the bride and groom, where it should be drawn.

Wedding announcements, on the other hand, are sent after the wedding has taken place. Therefore, it is necessary to include the year or it could be assumed that your wedding took place on any August twenty-third in the past.

The year can read either, "One thousand, nine hundred and ninety-seven" or "Nineteen hundred and ninety-seven."

Should the O *in "one thousand" and the* N *in "Nineteen hundred" be upper- or lowercase?*
Although both ways are proper and many older invitations use all lowercase letters on the year line, almost all invitations nowadays capitalize the first letter. This usage is so common that not to do it might make it look as though your stationer forgot to capitalize the first letter. Furthermore, your invitations will look more polished if the first letter of the year is capitalized.

Isn't it incorrect to use "and" as in "One thousand, nine hundred and ninety-seven"?

In mathematics "and" denotes a decimal point, and since there is no decimal point in the year "1997," it may seem incorrect to use "and." Wedding invitations, however, are not mathematical equations so the use of "and" as a decimal point is irrelevant. On wedding invitations "and" is used simply as a connective word.

TIME LINE

An old superstition claims that being married on the half hour brings good fortune since the minute hand is ascending toward heaven, while being married on the hour leads to a bad marriage since, as with the minute hand, it is all downhill from there. Perhaps it is best to be married at noon when the hands are in the praying position.

The time of the wedding is presented on one line and all letters are lowercase. If your wedding is being held at six o'clock, the time line simply reads, "at six o'clock." The time line for weddings held at six-thirty reads, "at half after six o'clock."

The time line can be used to designate the time of day by using either "in the morning," "in the afternoon," or "in the evening." For most times it is not usually necessary, since a wedding held at six o'clock, for example, is obviously being held in the evening. Weddings held at eight, nine, or ten o'clock are another matter, since they could be held in either the morning or the evening. In those cases, a designation denoting the time of day is helpful. In any event, you may always include the time of day if you find it aesthetically pleasing, and most older, traditional invitations do include it.

My wedding is being held at noon. Should my invitations read "at twelve o'clock noon"?

Your invitations should simply read, "at twelve o'clock." Unless otherwise noted, "twelve o'clock" means "noon."

If you feel strongly about indicating the time of day, you may use, "at twelve o'clock in the afternoon."

I am being married at 6:45. How should the time read?

The correct wording for 6:45 is "at three quarters after six o'clock." Although correct, the wording may appear awkward to many people, so it might be a good idea to change the time of your wedding to six-thirty or seven o'clock.

LOCATION

Wedding ceremonies are held at a variety of locations including churches, temples, synagogues, clubs, and even at home. The location line tells your guests the name of the location at which your wedding is being held. The full name of the facility is always given, so the location line for a wedding held at a church, for example, uses the full corporate name of the church. There should be no abbreviations. "Saint" is always spelled out. Likewise, a church commonly referred to as "Saint Matthew's Church" might actually be "Church of Saint Matthew" or "Saint Matthew's Roman Catholic Church." You should check with a clergyman or the church secretary to ascertain the correct name of the church.

My parents are hosting my wedding at home. How is that indicated?
While most wedding ceremonies are held in churches, hotels, and country clubs, many are held at home. The ceremony can be a religious one or a civil one. (Some religions, however, require that their wedding ceremonies be held in their place of worship.) The location given is simply your parents' address. Since your wedding is taking place outside a house of worship, "request the pleasure of your company" is used.

Mr. and Mrs. Andrew Jay Forrester

request the pleasure of your company

at the marriage of their daughter

Jennifer Marie

to

Mr. Nicholas Jude Strickland

Saturday, the twenty-third of August

at two o'clock

in the garden

2830 Meadowbrook Drive

Bedford, New York

We are having a garden wedding at my parents' home. Should our invitations indicate that it will be a garden wedding?

It is always helpful to mention that the wedding will be a garden wedding to ensure that your guests wear appropriate footwear. A line reading, "in the garden" appears above your parents' address.

Our wedding is being held at a friend's house. How does the location line read?

Your friend's name and address are shown at the end of the invitation.

Mr. and Mrs. Andrew Jay Forrester

request the pleasure of your company

at the marriage of their daughter

Jennifer Marie

to

Mr. Nicholas Jude Strickland

Saturday, the twenty-third of August

at six o'clock

at the residence of

Mr. and Mrs. Michael Anthony LaPointe

211 Old Orchard Road

Bedford, New York

and afterwards at the reception

**Our wedding is being held outdoors. How do we let our guests know
of our contingency plans in case of rain?**

One of the risks involved in having an outdoor wedding is that you are
at the mercy of the elements. You may enclose a small card with your
invitations that reads, "In case of inclement weather / the wedding will be
held at / Sleepy Hollow Country Club / Scarborough. Of course, all of
your guests will have different definitions of inclement weather. A cloudy
wedding day may produce a very large number of phone calls. If you are
planning an outdoor wedding, a tent would be a much wiser investment
than a bad-weather enclosure card.

*Our wedding is being held in a small chapel at the Church of Christ.
Is that noted on the invitations?*

The name of the chapel may be given on the line directly above the
name of the church.

STREET ADDRESS

The accepted rule on the use of the street address is that its inclusion is
optional unless there is more than one facility with that name in that
town, in which case it is mandatory. The street address is also used when
the facility is not well known or when there are a number of out-of-town
guests. Since giving the street address is an additional courtesy to your
guests, it is almost always proper. The only time its use is not proper is
when direction and map cards are used. Then the street address is redundant. Including the street address, however, adds an extra line to the
invitation. Most invitations, especially those engraved in script lettering
styles, look better with fewer lines of copy, so before you decide to include
the address consider the aesthetics.

CITY AND STATE

The last line in the main body of the invitation shows the names of the
city and state in which your wedding is being held. Both city and state
are included, and are separated by a comma.

Two exceptions to this rule are New York City and Washington, D.C.
For weddings held in New York, "New York City" or just "New York"
are used since "New York, New York" seems redundant. The city and
state line for weddings held in Washington, D.C. can read "in the city of
Washington" or "Washington, District of Columbia."

WEDDINGS AND RECEPTIONS HELD AT THE
SAME PLACE

When the wedding ceremony and reception are held in the same location, a line reading either "and afterwards at the reception" or "and
afterward at the reception" is included on the invitations. This line appears
at the end of the body of the invitation, beneath the city and state.

Many years ago, the reply request was engraved in the lower left-hand corner of invitations to weddings for which the ceremony and reception were held in the same place. This practice is gradually being replaced by reply cards and by reception cards, whose sole purpose is to give the reply information.

Mr. and Mrs. Andrew Jay Forrester

request the pleasure of your company

at the marriage of their daughter

Jennifer Marie

to

Mr. Nicholas Jude Strickland

Saturday, the twenty-third of August

at six o'clock

Sleepy Hollow Country Club

Scarborough, New York

and afterwards at the reception

My wedding and reception are being held at the same place. I do not want to send reply cards but I do not like the way corner lines look on wedding invitations. How should my reception cards read?

Although reception cards are not necessary in your situation, they may be used to convey your reply information. The reception cards read as they would if your reception were being held elsewhere. The name of the facility and its address, however, may be omitted since they are already given on the invitations.

HANDWRITTEN WEDDING INVITATIONS

For very small weddings involving only close friends and immediate family, handwritten invitations are the most personal way to invite your guests. Handwritten invitations take the form of a short note inviting your guests to your wedding. The wording varies, depending on your closeness to that guest. An invitation to somebody to whom you are rather close is written in a more familiar tone than one to a distant relative. The standard wedding format may be used when writing to somebody whom you do not know very well.

Handwritten invitations are written on plain, ecru or white letter sheets. (Letter sheets are sheets of stationery that have a fold on the left-hand side. They fold a second time from top to bottom to fit a single envelope.) While traditionally these sheets had no name or monogram on them, brides may now blind emboss their maiden name monogram at the top of the sheet.

The invitations should be written in black or dark blue ink.

Dear Aunt Kelly and Uncle Steven,

Nicholas and I will be getting married on Saturday, August Twenty-Third at six o'clock at the Church of Christ in Bedford. The reception will be held afterwards at the Club.

We want you to be a part of our wedding.

Love,
Jennifer

PERSONALIZED WEDDING INVITATIONS

The most formal wedding invitations are personalized. Personalized invitations are not only elegant, they honor your guests by showing them that you care enough about them to make their names a part of your wedding invitations.

Your guests' names are handwritten in black ink in a space reserved for them on the invitations. The handwriting on the invitations should match the handwriting used to address the envelopes.

Mr. and Mrs. Andrew Jay Forrester

request the honour of the presence of

Mr. and Mrs. Glenn Rougeau

at the marriage of their daughter

Jennifer Marie

etc.

When writing in our guests' names, what names do I use?

As on the mailing envelopes, your guests' full names and social titles are used. If you do not know a guest's middle name, it is omitted.

INVITATIONS ISSUED BY THE
GROOM'S PARENTS

On rare occasions, perhaps when the bride's parents are deceased or when they live in a foreign country, the groom's parents may issue the wedding invitations. The format is a little different from the standard format. The parents' relationship to the groom is mentioned on the fifth line of the invitation instead of on the third line. This way, the invitations can still be read as the bride being married to the groom. Both the bride and the groom use their full names, preceded by their titles.

Mr. and Mrs. John Peter Strickland

request the honour of your presence

at the marriage of

Miss Jennifer Marie Forrester

to their son

Mr. Nicholas Jude Strickland

etc.

INVITATIONS ISSUED BY OTHER RELATIVES

Any member of the bride's family may host her wedding and issue the invitations when the bride's parents are deceased. The bride's relationship to her relatives issuing the invitation is designated on the third line of the invitation where the word "daughter" normally appears. The bride's full name minus her title appears on the following line.

Mr. and Mrs. David Allen Forrester

request the honour of your presence

at the marriage of their granddaughter

Jennifer Marie Forrester

etc.

INVITATIONS ISSUED BY FRIENDS OF THE BRIDE

Friends of the bride may issue wedding invitations when the bride's parents are deceased and she has no close relatives. When friends issue the invitations, no relationship is shown on the third line and the bride's full name, preceded by "Miss," appears on the following line.

Mr. and Mrs. Charles Douglas Goldman

request the honour of your presence

at the marriage of

Miss Jennifer Marie Forrester

etc.

HISPANIC WEDDINGS

Traditional invitations to Hispanic weddings are issued by both sets of parents. The names of the bride's parents are always listed first.

Hispanic invitations can be done in a number of different formats. They may be engraved on one page, in English or Spanish, with the names of the bride's parents listed separately on the first two lines, "and" on the third line, and the names of the groom's parents listed on the following two lines.

They may also be engraved in both languages on the two inside pages of the invitations. The left inside page may be engraved in Spanish while the right inside page is engraved in English. When this format is used, the parents' names appear as described above.

Another frequently used format for Hispanic wedding invitations is an invitation engraved on the two inside pages on which the right-inside page is an invitation from the groom's parents and the left-inside page is an invitation from the bride's parents. Common copy, such as date, time, and place may be combined in the center of the invitation.

Customs may vary from one Latin American country to another. If you have any questions concerning the etiquette practiced in a particular country, it is best to call the protocol officer in their consulate for answers.

José Hernandez Caratini
Carmen María de Hernandez
y
Juan Martinez Garza
Consuela Elena de Martinez
tienen el honor de invitarle
al matrimonio de sus hijos
Linda
y
Roberto
el sabado diez de Julio
de mil novecientos noventa y siete
a las dos de la tarde
Santa Iglesia Catedral
San Juan de Puerto Rico

José Hernandez Caratini
Carmen Maria de Hernandez
request the honour of your presence
at the marriage of their daughter
Linda
to
Roberto Martinez

Juan Martinez Garza
Consuela Elena de Martinez
request the honour of your presence
at the marriage of
Linda Hernandez
to their son
Roberto

Saturday, the tenth of July
One thousand, nine hundred and ninety-seven
at two o'clock
Santa Iglesia Cathedral
San Juan, Puerto Rico

ROMAN CATHOLIC WEDDINGS

The Roman Catholic Church requires the posting of banns, the public announcement of a couple's intention to marry. The banns must be announced from the pulpit or in the church bulletin three times before the wedding. The traditional posting of the banns was the forerunner of today's wedding announcements.

Catholics can be married in a simple wedding service or in a Nuptial Mass. A Nuptial Mass is a wedding ceremony performed as part of a Catholic Mass (or service). When the wedding ceremony will be a Nuptial Mass, the invitations should mention that a Nuptial Mass will be performed. Nuptial Masses are about one hour long. Placing the phrase "Nuptial Mass" on the wedding invitations alerts guests to the fact that the wedding will take a little longer than what they might be accustomed to.

Nuptial Masses were once performed only at or before noon but are now performed in the afternoon as well. Unless special permission is granted by the bishop, Nuptial Masses may not be performed during Lent or Advent.

As suggested by the invitations, the bride and groom are joined together in holy matrimony. Therefore, "and" is used instead of "to."

Mr. and Mrs. Andrew Jay Forrester

request the honour of your presence

at the Nuptial Mass uniting their daughter

Jennifer Marie

and

Mr. Nicholas Jude Strickland

in the Sacrament of Holy Matrimony

Saturday, the twenty-third of August

at nine o'clock in the morning

Saint Matthew's Roman Catholic Church

Bedford, New York

JEWISH WEDDINGS

According to Jewish tradition, marriages are made in heaven. Men and women are brought together to marry one another by God himself. Women are not married "to" men. Rather, men and women are joined together in marriage. Because of this tradition, the joining word on Jewish wedding invitations reads "and" instead of "to."

Jewish custom also celebrates the joining of the two families, so the names of the groom's parents always appear on the invitations. Their names most properly appear beneath the groom's name on a line reading "son of Mr. and Mrs. Solomon Lang" or on two lines that read, "son of / Mr. and Mrs. Solomon Lang." Their names may also appear at the top of the invitations beneath the names of the bride's parents. This is done occasionally by parents of the bride who feel that they honor the groom's parents more by placing their names at the top of the invitation. When this is done, the request line reads, "at the marriage of." The bride, in this case, uses her full name but no title. The groom's title is omitted as well to maintain uniformity.

Hebrew lettering is often used on Jewish wedding invitations. It may take the form of a quotation from the wedding blessing, blind embossed across the top of the invitation, or the entire invitation text may be reproduced on a part of the invitation. When the invitation appears in both English and Hebrew, the Hebrew version appears on the left-inside page while the English version appears on the right-inside page.

Mr. and Mrs. David Green

request the honour of your presence

at the marriage of their daughter

Deborah

to

Mr. Steven Lang

son of

Mr. and Mrs. Solomon Lang

Sunday, the twenty-fourth of August

at six o'clock

Temple Beth-el

Scarsdale, New York

Mr. and Mrs. David Green
Mr. and Mrs. Solomon Lang
request the honour of your presence
at the marriage of
Deborah Green
and
Steven Lang
etc.

Is it proper to use "at the marriage of their children"?

While it is equally correct to use "at the marriage of their children" and "at the marriage of," many people feel that if a couple is old enough to get married, they are no longer children.

MORMON WEDDINGS

Members of the Church of Jesus Christ of Latter-day Saints are married or "sealed" for "time and eternity" in temples open only to practicing Latter-day Saints. Weddings are generally small and intimate, attended by family and very close friends. The reception afterwards is a much larger affair to which all friends and all members of the bride's and groom's extended families are invited. Since more guests are invited to the reception than to the ceremony, the invitations are for the reception. Ceremony cards enclosed with the reception invitations are sent to those guests who are also invited to the temple ceremony.

Invitations to Latter-day Saint wedding receptions differ from standard reception invitations in that they mention that the wedding ceremony was performed in a Latter-day Saint temple. Because Latter-day Saints place great emphasis on the importance of families, the groom's parents are honored by having their names mentioned on wedding invitations. Their names appear beneath the groom's name, preceded by "son of" on a

RECEPTION INVITATION:

Mr. and Mrs. Andrew Jay Forrester
request the pleasure of your company
at the marriage reception of their daughter
Jennifer Marie
and
Mr. Nicholas Jude Strickland
son of
Mr. and Mrs. John Peter Strickland
following their marriage
in the Salt Lake L.D.S. Temple
Saturday, the twenty-third of August
from seven until nine o'clock
La Caille at Quail Run
Salt Lake City, Utah

separate line. Guests drop in and out of Latter-day Saint receptions. They arrive to congratulate the newlyweds and stay for a while to talk to friends and to renew acquaintances. Then they leave and go on their way. Consequently, the time line on the invitations mentions the time period during which the reception will be held.

Ceremony cards draw a distinction between weddings held in a Mormon temple and weddings held elsewhere. When weddings are held in a temple, it is so noted on the ceremony card.

CEREMONY CARD:

The honour of your presence is requested
at the Temple Ceremony
Saturday, the twenty-third of August
at six o'clock
Salt Lake Temple

Is it proper for us to send a photograph of ourselves with our wedding invitations?

While most Latter-day Saints do send their photographs with their invitations, it is not proper to do so. The principal purpose of wedding invitations is to invite guests to your wedding. Anything else is superfluous. You may, of course, send photos in a separate mailing.

MILITARY WEDDINGS

Invitations to weddings involving members of the United States armed services follow the same general guidelines used for civilian weddings. The format and the wording are the same. The only difference is in the use of titles. While civilians use social titles such as "Mr.," "Mrs.," and "Doctor," military personnel use their military titles, which many times include their rank and branch of service. Military titles should not be abbreviated.

Officers in the army, air force, and marines with a rank of captain or higher use their military titles before their names. Navy and coast guard officers with a rank of commander or higher also use their military titles before their names. When officers' names are used by themselves, the name of the branch of service in which they serve is mentioned on the line beneath their names. When their names are used with their spouse's name, the branch of service is not mentioned.

Junior officers do not use titles (neither military nor civilian) before their names. Their titles appear on a second line before the name of their branch of service. First lieutenants and Second lieutenants in the army both use "Lieutenant." In the air force and marines, however, "First" and "Second" are used.

All other members of the military use only their branch of service on a second line. Their ranks are not used.

High-ranking officers who retire generally continue to use their military titles. Their retired status is noted after their service designation. When the service designation is not used, as on invitations issued by a retired colonel and his wife, the officer's retired status is not mentioned.

PARENTS OF THE BRIDE

Parents Are Married

FATHER IS AN OFFICER
Colonel and Mrs. Andrew Jay Forrester

FATHER IS A JUNIOR OFFICER
Lieutenant and Mrs. Andrew Jay Forrester

FATHER IS A NONCOMMISSIONED OFFICER OR ENLISTED MAN
Mr. and Mrs. Andrew Jay Forrester

FATHER IS A RETIRED OFFICER
Colonel and Mrs. Andrew Jay Forrester

MOTHER IS AN OFFICER
Mrs. and Mrs. Andrew Jay Forrester
    or
Captain Mary Chance Forrester
United States Army
and Mr. Andrew Jay Forrester

BOTH PARENTS ARE OFFICERS
Colonel and Mrs. Andrew Jay Forrester
    or
Captain Mary Chance Forrester
United States Army
and Colonel Andrew Jay Forrester
United States Army

BOTH PARENTS HOLD THE SAME RANK
Colonel and Mrs. Andrew Jay Forrester
   or
The Colonels Forrester
   or
Colonel Mary Chance Forrester
United States Army
and Colonel Andrew Jay Forrester
United States Army

Parents Are Divorced

FATHER IS AN OFFICER
Mrs. Mary Chance Forrester
Colonel Andrew Jay Forrester
United States Army

FATHER IS A JUNIOR OFFICER
Mrs. Mary Chance Forrester
Andrew Jay Forrester
Lieutenant, United States Army

FATHER IS A NONCOMMISSIONED OFFICER OR ENLISTED MAN
Mrs. Mary Chance Forrester
Andrew Jay Forrester
United States Army

FATHER IS A RETIRED OFFICER
Mrs. Mary Chance Forrester
Colonel Andrew Jay Forrester
United States Army, Retired

MOTHER IS AN OFFICER
Captain Mary Chance Forrester
United States Army
Mr. Andrew Jay Forrester

BRIDE'S NAME

OFFICER
Commander Jennifer Marie Forrester
United States Navy

JUNIOR OFFICER
Jennifer Marie Forrester
Ensign, United States Navy

NONCOMMISSIONED OFFICER OR ENLISTED WOMAN
Jennifer Marie Forrester
United States Navy

GROOM'S NAME

OFFICER
Major Nicholas Jude Strickland
United States Marine Corps

JUNIOR OFFICER
Nicholas Jude Strickland
First Lieutenant, United States Marine Corps

NONCOMMISSIONED OFFICER OR ENLISTED MAN
Nicholas Jude Strickland
United States Marine Corps

POSTPONEMENT OF A WEDDING

Weddings are occasionally postponed due to illness or an unexpected death in the family. When there is enough time to do so, formal announcements are mailed to invited guests. The announcements are engraved or printed on formal wedding stationery that matches the original wedding invitations. Postponement announcements announce the postponement and give the new wedding date. If there is not enough time to send announcements by mail, guests may be notified by phone.

Mr. and Mrs. Andrew Jay Forrester

announce that the marriage of their daughter

Jennifer Marie

to

Mr. Nicholas Jude Strickland

has been postponed to

Saturday, the twentieth of September

at six o'clock

Church of Christ

Bedford, New York

RECALLING WEDDING INVITATIONS

Wedding invitations are recalled when a wedding needs to be postponed before a new wedding date has been set. Recalling invitations officially cancels them so new invitations must be issued to reinvite your guests once a new date is set.

The recall notices and the new invitations should match the original invitations. The reason that the invitations are being recalled is usually mentioned. If there is not enough time to send recall notices, you may notify your guests by phone.

RECALL NOTICE:

Mr. and Mrs. Andrew Jay Forrester

regret that the illness of their daughter

Jennifer Marie

obliges them to recall their invitations

to her marriage to

Mr. Nicholas Jude Strickland

on Saturday, the twenty-third of August

NEW INVITATION:

Mr. and Mrs. Andrew Jay Forrester

announce that the wedding of their daughter

Jennifer Marie

to

Mr. Nicholas Jude Strickland

which was postponed, will now take place

on Saturday, the twentieth of September

at six o'clock

Church of Christ

Bedford, New York

CANCELING A WEDDING

When a wedding needs to be canceled, formal announcements may be sent. Cancelation announcements should match the wedding invitations. If there is not enough time to send a formal announcement, phone calls may be made instead.

Mr. and Mrs. Andrew Jay Forrester

are obliged to recall their invitations

to the marriage of their daughter

Jennifer Marie

to

Mr. Nicholas Jude Strickland

as the marriage will not take place

INVITATIONS TO THE RECEPTION

Wedding ceremonies and receptions do not necessarily have the same number of guests. Many couples, especially those in which the bride is a second-time bride, have small, intimate ceremonies with larger receptions afterwards. Since more people are invited to the reception than to the ceremony, the invitations are for the reception. Guests invited to the ceremony are sent ceremony cards with their reception invitations.

Reception invitations always "request the pleasure of your company" since the reception is not being held in a house of worship. The word "and" is used to join the names of the bride and groom. The phrases "marriage reception" and "wedding reception" are both correct. "Marriage reception" is the more traditional of the two but many brides prefer "wedding reception," arguing that a wedding is the act of getting married while marriage is the result of that decision.

RECEPTION INVITATION:

Mr. and Mrs. Andrew Jay Forrester

request the pleasure of your company

at the marriage reception of their daughter

Jennifer Marie

and

Mr. Nicholas Jude Strickland

Saturday, the twenty-third of August

at seven o'clock

Sleepy Hollow Country Club

Scarborough, New York

CEREMONY CARD:

The honour of your presence is requested

at the marriage ceremony

Saturday, the twenty-third of August

at six o'clock

Church of Christ

Bedford

LATE RECEPTIONS

Wedding receptions take place on the day of the wedding. Any reception occurring after that date is not properly referred to as a wedding reception. Rather, it is a party or reception in honor of the recently married couple.

These receptions are held for a variety of reasons. Most late receptions are held when the bride and her family live in different parts of the country. Others, especially those involving older couples or second-time brides, may hold late receptions due to professional considerations. Whatever the reason, late receptions are becoming a more common occurrence.

Invitations to a late reception contain a line reading, "in honour of" or "in honor of" followed on a separate line with the names of the couple.

Mr. and Mrs. Andrew Jay Forrester

request the pleasure of your company

at a dinner reception

in honor of

Mr. and Mrs. Nicholas Jude Strickland

Saturday, the twentieth of September

at seven o'clock

Sleepy Hollow Country Club

Scarborough, New York

We are having a small ceremony for just our families in August. We are also planning a reception in September. Is it proper to send our reception invitations with our wedding announcements?

Invitations are never properly sent with announcements. Your wedding and your late reception are separate events that require separate mailings.

We are having a small reception immediately following our wedding and a larger reception a month later. May we enclose a reception card for our late reception?

Receptions that take place after the wedding day are not considered wedding receptions. They are simply parties in honor of the couple. The party is an event that is not a part of your wedding, so it requires separate invitations and a separate mailing.

WEDDING ANNIVERSARIES

While wedding anniversaries are observed every year, major celebrations are usually reserved for the twenty-fifth, fortieth, and fiftieth anniversaries. Formal invitations to wedding anniversaries should be engraved on letter sheets. You do not need to use black ink and may, instead, use silver for a twenty-fifth anniversary, red for a fortieth anniversary, and gold for a fiftieth wedding anniversary.

Invitations to wedding anniversaries are usually extended by the couple's children and their spouses, but friends, grandchildren, and even the couple themselves may issue them as well. The years of their marriage may be shown at the top of the invitation. A line reading, "No gifts, please" may appear in the lower right-hand corner or, better yet, a card reading, "Your presence is the only gift we request" may be sent with the invitations. If reply cards are not being used, the reply information is given in the lower left-hand corner.

1947 – 1997

Mr. and Mrs. Nicholas Jude Strickland, junior

Mr. and Mrs. Robert Stuart Strickland

Mr. and Mrs. John Kevin Murphey

request the pleasure of your company

at a dinner to celebrate

the Fiftieth Wedding Anniversary of

Mr. and Mrs. Nicholas Jude Strickland

Saturday, the fifth of April

at seven o'clock

Sleepy Hollow Country Club

Scarborough, New York

TRADITIONAL ANNIVERSARY GIFTS

1.	Paper	13.	Lace
2.	Cotton	14.	Ivory
3.	Leather	15.	Crystal
4.	Silk	20.	China
5.	Wood	25.	Silver
6.	Iron	30.	Pearls
7.	Copper or wool	35.	Coral and jade
8.	Electrical appliances	40.	Ruby
9.	Pottery	45.	Sapphire
10.	Tin or aluminum	50.	Gold
11.	Steel	75.	Diamond
12.	Linen		

REAFFIRMATION OF WEDDING VOWS

A number of married couples choose to celebrate their anniversaries by having a ceremony to renew their wedding vows. Other couples, married in a civil ceremony for one reason or another, choose to reaffirm their vows under religious auspices. As with any other invitation, invitations to reaffirmation ceremonies should reflect the formality of the occasion.

Mr. and Mrs. Nicholas Jude Strickland

request the honour of your presence

at a ceremony to celebrate

the reaffirmation of their wedding vows

Saturday, the twenty-third of August

at six o'clock

Church of Christ

Bedford, New York

and at a reception afterwards

Sleepy Hollow Country Club

Scarborough

My father became ill a couple of months before I was supposed to be married. Instead of the large church ceremony that we planned, my fiancé and I were married in my father's hospital room. We would still like to be married in our church. How should our invitations read?

Your invitations may be issued by either your mother or by you and your fiancé. If you were married in a religious ceremony, your invitations would read as a reaffirmation of your wedding vows. If, however, you were married in a civil ceremony and now wish to get married in a religious ceremony, your invitations would state that the ceremony was being performed to solemnize your marriage. (To solemnize means to make right before God.)

Mrs. Andrew Jay Forrester
requests the honour of your presence
at the religious ceremony to solemnize
the marriage of her daughter
Jennifer Marie
and
Mr. Nicholas Jude Strickland
etc.

WEDDING ANNOUNCEMENTS

Weddings are traditionally announced by the bride's parents, who may send announcements to relatives and friends not sent invitations to the wedding. They are sent after the wedding has taken place, never before. When circumstances permit, announcements are sent the day after the wedding. If the newlyweds eloped or the decision to send announcements was made late, the announcements may still be sent—any time up to one year afterwards is acceptable.

Wedding announcements follow the same format as the invitations. They are engraved in black ink on ecru or white letter sheets. If wedding invitations are being sent, the announcements match the invitations. Many brides, however, send their announcements on stationery that is smaller than the stationery used for their invitations. There is no point of etiquette that suggests this as being more proper. Rather, it is a matter of personal preference. Like the invitations, wedding announcements are mailed in double envelopes. They are addressed using the same etiquette that is used for addressing wedding invitation envelopes.

The bride's parents "have the honour of announcing" the marriage. "Have the honour to announce" may also be used. A less formal phrase, "announce the marriage of their daughter," is occasionally used, although its use may be misconstrued as suggesting that the bride's parents disapprove of the marriage (since "honour" is not mentioned).

Since wedding announcements are sent after the wedding has taken place, they announce a past event. Therefore, the year is always included. It is written out on its own line following the date as either "One thousand, nine hundred and ninety-seven" or "Nineteen hundred and ninety-seven." If the wedding was held in a church, temple, or synagogue, the name of the house of worship is mentioned beneath the year.

Wedding announcements may also be sent by the bride and groom themselves. The bride's name and title appear on the first line. "And" constitutes the second line. The groom's name appears on line three. The bride and groom simply announce their marriage. They do not "have the honour" of doing so since that would be presumptuous. Neither do they "joyfully" announce since their happiness is assumed.

Most wedding announcements are sent with at-home cards. At-home cards are small enclosure cards on which your address is given.

ISSUED BY THE BRIDE'S PARENTS:

Mr. and Mrs. Andrew Jay Forrester

have the honour of announcing

the marriage of their daughter

Jennifer Marie

to

Mr. Nicholas Jude Strickland

Saturday, the twenty-third of August

One thousand, nine hundred and ninety-seven

Church of Christ

Bedford, New York

ISSUED BY THE BRIDE AND GROOM:

Miss Jennifer Marie Forrester

and

Mr. Nicholas Jude Strickland

announce their marriage

Saturday, the twenty-third of August

One thousand, nine hundred and ninety-seven

Church of Christ

Bedford, New York

We are having a small wedding. I would like to send announcements but I don't want anybody to think I'm asking for a gift.

Wedding announcements simply announce the fact that you have gotten married. They do not require their recipients to send gifts. Neither does the inclusion of an at-home card. At-home cards merely make it easier for your family and friends to stay in touch with you.

When should I order my wedding announcements?

Since wedding announcements are sent anytime from the day after the wedding until one year later, you have plenty of leeway in ordering your announcements. Most brides, however, order their announcements when they order their invitations. If you are not ordering wedding invitations, you should order your announcements as soon as you have all the pertinent information so they can be mailed as soon after your wedding as possible.

We are having a small wedding in August and a large reception in September. Is it proper to enclose a reception card with our announcements?

Invitations to a late reception should not be sent with your announcements. Your wedding and your late reception are separate events. They therefore require separate mailings.

ADDRESSING THE ENVELOPES

Wedding invitations were once delivered by hand. If you were a bride back in those days, your footman delivered your invitations to your guests' homes. Their servants received the invitations and removed them from their mailing envelope, an envelope much too pedestrian for your guests to handle themselves. The servants, then, presented the invitation to your guests in its pristine inside envelope. Because the invitations were already at their destination, the inside envelopes had only the names of your guests written on them. The address was no longer needed. They just had to be directed to the appropriate members of the household.

Wedding invitations are still sent in two envelopes. The outside envelope is the mailing envelope. No abbreviations are used. "Rural Route" and "Post Office Box" are always written out.

Your guests' names and addresses are written on its face. The copy may be centered or staggered. Staggered copy was much more popular years ago before there was such a thing as zip codes and before it was necessary to include the state on invitations sent in-state. Now, the addition of states and zip codes has, in most cases, made the last line too long to be staggered.

Your guests' names are repeated on the inside envelope. This time, however, only their titles and surnames are used. If children under the age of eighteen are invited, their first names would appear on a line beneath their parents' names.

The back flap of the outside envelope has the sender's address blind embossed or engraved on it. Blind embossing is the more traditional of the two. It is preferred over engraving because of the feeling that the first time guests see the engraving, it should be on the beautifully engraved invitations. The return address, on the other hand, should melt into the background. The post office disagrees. They prefer engraving since it is easier to read. The postal service would also like you to engrave the return address in the upper left corner of the envelope's face. Don't do it. It will make your invitations look too commercial.

Only the address is blind embossed on the envelope flaps. The names are not. The apartment number must be given when applicable, since without the name there would be no way of identifying the sender. The apartment may appear alone on the first line with "Apartment" spelled out or at the end of the street address, preceded by a comma or a bullet. (A bullet is a period that is raised to a point halfway between the top and the bottom of a line.)

The address of whoever issued the invitations appears on the back flap. If, for example, your parents issued your invitations, their address appears. Many people, however, use the return address as an indication of where the gifts should be sent, so if you would like to have your presents sent directly to you, you may use your address for the return address.

If you have nice handwriting, you may address the envelopes yourself. If not, you may hire a calligrapher instead. Calligraphy is a centuries-old art that was practiced in monasteries by monks who copied Bibles and other important documents by hand. Copying books and documents by hand eventually all but ceased as printing and engraving replaced the scribe. Indeed, many of the lettering styles available in engraving can be traced back to old calligraphic styles. Calligraphy is still practiced today and gives your wedding envelopes a charming Old World look.

Wedding envelopes are addressed using the same etiquette that is used on wedding invitations. Because they are seen only by their recipients, less traditional etiquette is occasionally used, especially with women's names and titles. "Ms.," for example, may be used when addressing envelopes even though it is not properly used on invitations.

Wedding envelopes are addressed in black ink to match the invitations.

MARRIED COUPLE

OUTSIDE ENVELOPE
Mr. and Mrs. Troy Clayton

INSIDE ENVELOPE
Mr. and Mrs. Clayton

with Children under Eighteen Living at Home
OUTSIDE ENVELOPE
Mr. and Mrs. Troy Clayton

INSIDE ENVELOPE
Mr. and Mrs. Clayton
Marvin and Heather

with Two Daughters over Eighteen Living at Home
OUTSIDE ENVELOPE
The Misses Clayton
or
Miss Heather Clayton
Miss Mindy Clayton

INSIDE ENVELOPE
The Misses Clayton

with Two Sons under Eighteen Living at Home
OUTSIDE ENVELOPE
The Messrs. Clayton
or
Mr. Lawrence Clayton
Mr. Kevin Clayton

INSIDE ENVELOPE
The Messrs. Clayton

with a Son and a Daughter over Eighteen Living at Home
OUTSIDE ENVELOPE
Miss Heather Clayton
Mr. Marvin Clayton

INSIDE ENVELOPE
Miss Clayton
Mr. Clayton

in Which Woman Kept Maiden Name
OUTSIDE ENVELOPE
Ms. Christine Pritchett
and Mr. Troy Clayton

INSIDE ENVELOPE
Ms. Pritchett
and Mr. Clayton

in Which Man Is a Doctor
OUTSIDE ENVELOPE
Doctor and Mrs. Troy Clayton

INSIDE ENVELOPE
Doctor and Mrs. Clayton

in Which Both Are Doctors

OUTSIDE ENVELOPE	INSIDE ENVELOPE
Doctor and Mrs. Troy Clayton	Doctor and Mrs. Clayton
or	or
The Doctors Clayton	The Doctors Clayton
or	
Doctor Christine Clayton	
and Doctor Troy Clayton	

in Which Woman Is a Doctor

OUTSIDE ENVELOPE	INSIDE ENVELOPE
Mr. and Mrs. Troy Clayton	Mr. and Mrs. Clayton
or	or
Doctor Christine Clayton	Doctor Clayton
and Mr. Troy Clayton	and Mr. Clayton

in Which Man Is a Judge

OUTSIDE ENVELOPE	INSIDE ENVELOPE
The Honorable and Mrs. Troy Clayton	Judge and Mrs. Clayton

in Which Woman Is a Judge

OUTSIDE ENVELOPE	INSIDE ENVELOPE
Mr. and Mrs. Troy Clayton	Mr. and Mrs. Clayton
or	or
The Honorable Christine Clayton	Judge Clayton
and Mr. Troy Clayton	and Mr. Clayton

in Which One or Both Members Are Lawyers

OUTSIDE ENVELOPE	INSIDE ENVELOPE
Mr. and Mrs. Troy Clayton	Mr. and Mrs. Clayton

UNMARRIED COUPLE LIVING TOGETHER

OUTSIDE ENVELOPE	INSIDE ENVELOPE
Miss Christine Pritchett	Miss Pritchett
Mr. Troy Clayton	Mr. Clayton
or	or
Ms. Christine Pritchett	Ms. Pritchett
Mr. Troy Clayton	Mr. Clayton

DIVORCED WOMAN

OUTSIDE ENVELOPE	INSIDE ENVELOPE
Mrs. Christine Pritchett Clayton	Mrs. Clayton
or	or
Ms. Christine Pritchett Clayton	Ms. Clayton

Who Has Resumed Using Maiden Name

OUTSIDE ENVELOPE	INSIDE ENVELOPE
Ms. Christine Pritchett	Ms. Pritchett

WIDOW

OUTSIDE ENVELOPE	INSIDE ENVELOPE
Mrs. Troy Clayton	Mrs. Clayton

SINGLE WOMAN

OUTSIDE ENVELOPE	INSIDE ENVELOPE
Miss Christine Pritchett	Miss Pritchett
or	or
Ms. Christine Pritchett	Ms. Pritchett

and Date

OUTSIDE ENVELOPE	INSIDE ENVELOPE
Miss Christine Pritchett	Miss Pritchett and escort
or	or
Ms. Christine Pritchett	Miss Pritchett and guest
	or
	Ms. Pritchett and escort
	or
	Ms. Pritchett and guest

SINGLE MAN

OUTSIDE ENVELOPE	INSIDE ENVELOPE
Mr. Troy Clayton	Mr. Clayton

and Date

OUTSIDE ENVELOPE
Mr. Troy Clayton

INSIDE ENVELOPE
Mr. Clayton and guest

MILITARY TITLES *

* Please note that the service designation should always appear on the same line with the name and rank. In the following entries, service designations that appear on separate lines do so to accommodate space limitations.

MARRIED COUPLES

in Which Man Is an Officer

OUTSIDE ENVELOPE
Colonel and Mrs. Troy Clayton

INSIDE ENVELOPE
Colonel and Mrs. Clayton

in Which Man Is a Noncommissioned Officer or Enlisted Man

OUTSIDE ENVELOPE
Mr. and Mrs. Troy Clayton

INSIDE ENVELOPE
Mr. and Mrs. Clayton

in Which Man Is a Retired Officer

OUTSIDE ENVELOPE
Colonel and Mrs. Troy Clayton

INSIDE ENVELOPE
Colonel and Mrs. Clayton

in Which Woman Is an Officer

OUTSIDE ENVELOPE
Mr. and Mrs. Troy Clayton
or
Captain Christine Clayton,
U.S. Army
and Mr. Troy Clayton

INSIDE ENVELOPE
Mr. and Mrs. Clayton
or
Captain Clayton
and Mr. Troy Clayton

in Which Both Are Officers

OUTSIDE ENVELOPE	INSIDE ENVELOPE
Colonel and Mrs. Troy Clayton	Colonel and Mrs. Clayton
or	or
Captain Christine Clayton,	Captain Clayton
U.S. Army	and Colonel Clayton
and Colonel Troy Clayton,	
U.S. Army	

SINGLE WOMAN

Who Is an Officer

OUTSIDE ENVELOPE	INSIDE ENVELOPE
Captain Christine Pritchett,	Captain Pritchett
U.S. Army	

Who Is a Junior Officer

OUTSIDE ENVELOPE	INSIDE ENVELOPE
Lieutenant Christine Pritchett,	Lieutenant Pritchett
U.S. Army	

Who Is a Noncommissioned Officer or Enlisted Woman

OUTSIDE ENVELOPE	INSIDE ENVELOPE
Miss Christine Pritchett	Miss Pritchett
or	or
Ms. Christine Pritchett	Ms. Pritchett

SINGLE MAN

Who Is an Officer

OUTSIDE ENVELOPE	INSIDE ENVELOPE
Colonel Troy Clayton, U.S. Army	Colonel Clayton

Who Is a Junior Officer

OUTSIDE ENVELOPE	INSIDE ENVELOPE
Lieutenant Troy Clayton,	Lieutenant Clayton
U.S. Army	

Who Is a Noncommissioned Officer or Enlisted Man

OUTSIDE ENVELOPE   INSIDE ENVELOPE
Mr. Troy Clayton   Mr. Clayton

We are sending wedding invitations to two sisters who are living together. Whose name is first?

When addressing envelopes to two or more siblings under the age of eighteen who are living at home, the name of the oldest child is listed first followed by the names of his or her siblings in reverse chronological order. If they are over eighteen, they receive separate invitations.

We are sending wedding invitations to a couple with two children. Do we use "and family" on the outside envelope?

No. Wedding invitations are sent to the adult members of the household. In your case, the outside envelope is addressed to the parents who receive the invitations on behalf of their children. Their children's names (not "and family"), if you wish to invite them, are written on the inside envelope on a line beneath the names of their parents.

We are sending invitations to a "junior." Do we use "junior"?

If "junior" is a part of a man's name, you would include it (or "Jr.") on the outside envelope. It is not necessary to repeat it on the inside envelope unless both "junior" and "senior" are living at the same address.

Should we use numerals or should we write out the numbers?

Numerals are usually used for the street number, although it is also appropriate to write out numbers one through twenty. Numbered streets may appear whichever way is more aesthetically pleasing. Numerals are always used for zip codes.

How can I tell which envelopes are the mailing envelopes?

It is easy to tell which envelopes are which. The outside envelopes have glue on them; the inside envelopes do not and they are also a bit smaller. To avoid confusion when addressing envelopes, it is best to work with one set of envelopes at a time. Address all the outside envelopes first. After those are all addressed, start addressing the inside envelopes. That will make it almost impossible to address the wrong envelopes.

I am addressing an envelope to a man and woman who are living together. Whose name goes first?
The woman's name goes first.

A number of our friends are seeing somebody. We would like to invite them to our wedding. How is that done?
The nicest way to invite dates is to call your friends, get the names of their dates, and send them each an invitation. A less formal way is to address the inside envelopes with either "Mr. Clayton and guest" or "Miss Clayton and escort." Women who feel that an escort is unnecessary in this day and age prefer "Miss Clayton and guest" or "Ms. Clayton and guest."

ASSEMBLING THE INVITATIONS

Your wedding invitations may arrive already stuffed into their inner envelopes or in separate stacks of invitations, enclosure cards, and inner and outer envelopes. If yours come unassembled, there is no need to panic. Assembling wedding invitations is really quite simple, albeit time consuming.

For the most part, wedding invitations are assembled in size order. The invitation itself is first. The enclosure cards are stacked on top of the invitations, not inside. The reception card is placed on top of the invitation. Then the reply envelope is placed face down on the reception card. The reply card is slipped face up beneath the flap of the reply envelope. These are the most frequently used enclosures. Any other enclosures are added face up in size order (usually at-home card, direction card, accommodation card, pew card, etc.).

The single-fold invitation and its enclosures are placed into the inside envelope with the fold of the invitation at the bottom of the envelope and the engraving facing the back of the envelope. You can tell whether or not you stuffed the envelope correctly by removing the invitation with your right hand. If you can read the invitation without turning it, it was stuffed correctly.

The procedure for assembling traditional invitations (those with a second fold) is similar. The enclosures are placed on top of the lower half of the invitation's face in the same order described above. The invitation is folded from top to bottom over the enclosures. The invitation is then placed into the inside envelope with the fold toward the bottom of the envelope. As with other invitations, traditional invitations are correctly stuffed when they can be read, without being turned, after being removed from the envelope with your right hand.

Once stuffed, the inside envelopes are inserted into the outside envelopes. The front of the inside envelope faces the back of the outside envelope.

My invitations came with tissues. Should I send them or remove them?

All wedding invitations were once shipped with small pieces of tissue separating each invitation. This prevented the slow-drying ink from smudging. Before mailing her invitations, the bride removed the tissues as they were merely packing material and served no point of etiquette. Through the years, many brides, unaware of the impropriety of sending tissued invitations, left the tissues in. As this practice grew, tissued invitations became as proper as nontissued invitations.

Today, wedding invitations are properly sent both ways. Tissues are starting to serve an important function again as the postal service's sorting equipment can cause smudging on invitations sent without tissues. If you are sending invitations without tissues, you may be able to ask your local post office to hand cancel them. Hand canceling also prevents the postal service from printing their advertising, disguised as a part of the cancelation mark, on your wedding invitations.

Where are the tissues placed?

Since the tissues are meant to prevent smudging, they should be placed over the copy on each invitation and enclosure.

1. *A single-fold invitation
inserted into an envelope*

2. *Inserting a single-fold invitation
with an enclosure card*

3. *A twice-fold invitation
inserted into an envelope*

4. *Inserting a twice-folded invitation
with an enclosure card*

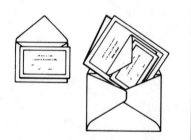

5. *Enclosing a reply card and envelope*

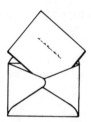

6. *Placing an inner envelope
into an outer envelope*

RECEPTION CARDS

Reception cards are used whenever the wedding ceremony and reception are held in different places. Because they are at different locations, they are considered separate events. Therefore, they each require their own invitations. Reception cards are not necessary when the ceremony and the reception are held at the same place.

The first line on the reception card indicates the occasion. It reads "Breakfast" when occurring before one o'clock (regardless of the menu) and "Reception" when held at one o'clock or later.

The next line indicates the time and usually reads, "immediately following the ceremony." This phrase should not be taken literally as it simply means that the reception will start in, more or less, the amount of time it takes to get from the ceremony to the reception. If the reception is scheduled to start two or more hours after the ceremony ends, the phrase "immediately following the ceremony" should be replaced with the appropriate time. The line may then read, "at eight o'clock."

The name of the facility at which the reception will take place is given on the third line. The address is usually shown on a fourth line, although it is omitted whenever the facility is very well known or when direction and map cards are used.

The city and state follow on the next line if they are not the same as those shown on the invitation. If the city and state do not appear on the reception card, it is assumed that the reception is in the same town as the wedding, Likewise, if the city is different but the state is the same, you need only mention the city. These are options. You may, however, under any circumstances use both city and state.

When reply cards are not being sent, a reply is requested in the lower left-hand corner of the reception card. Corner lines are engraved in a smaller size than the body of the reception card.

The top line asks your guests to reply by stating either, "The favour of a reply is requested," "R.s.v.p.," or "R.S.V.P." All three are considered proper. However, in some regions, such as the southern United States "The favour of a reply is requested" is preferred while "R.s.v.p." is frowned upon.

The address to which the replies are to be sent is shown on the following two lines. The address shown is the address of the person whose name first appears on the wedding invitation. So if the invitation was issued by your parents, the lines would contain your parents' address. If you would like to have the replies sent to you, you must put your name, preceded by your title, on the lines beneath the reply request.

Whether you use your address or your parents' address, you should always include an address on your reception cards to reply to even when the same address appears on the invitation's outside envelope (except when also sending reply cards). People tend to discard envelopes, especially when there is an additional inside envelope. If some of your guests throw out their envelopes and there is no address inside, they may not be able to reply. This could result in your having to make some unnecessary phone calls.

Reception

immediately following the ceremony

Sleepy Hollow Country Club

Scarborough, New York

The favour of a reply is requested
2830 Meadowbrook Drive
Bedford, New York 10506

What is the correct spelling of "favor"?

Both "favor" and "favour" are correct. Like "honor" and "honour," it is a matter of personal preference, although the vast majority of brides prefer the English spelling, "favour." If you use the English spelling of "honour," use the English spelling of "favour" also, for consistency.

My wedding reception will include a sit-down dinner. How is that indicated?

In most cases, no special designation is made. Many brides, however, worry that their guests might not know that a meal will be served and will make other plans for dinner. You may alert your guests about the dinner by engraving, "Dinner Reception" on the top line of your reception cards.

How do I let my guests know that there will be dancing at the reception?

While some brides use "Dinner and Dancing" on the first line of their reception cards, it is usually not necessary to do so. If there is a band and a dance floor, people will dance.

Although we love our nieces and nephews, we would rather not have any children at our wedding. How can we nicely tell our guests that their children are not invited?

The names of the family members that you are inviting are written on the inside envelope. If children are not invited to your wedding, their names are simply left off the inside envelope. Thus, when "Mr. and Mrs. Sterling" is written on the inside envelope, it means that only Mr. and Mrs. Sterling are invited, not their children. If their children were to be invited, the inside envelope would read:

Mr. and Mrs. Sterling

Kathryn, Robby, and John

Of course most people are not familiar with this point of etiquette and a corner line reading, "No children, please" seems a bit cruel, so what else can you do? The best solution is to talk to your family members and friends with children and let them know that, although you would really love to invite their children, expenses (or whatever) prevent you from doing so. A possible compromise might be to invite children to the ceremony but not to the reception. This, too, is best handled by talking it over with those involved.

We are having a formal reception. Where do the words "Black tie" appear?

The words, "Black tie" do not properly appear on wedding invitations or reception cards. The time of day and the location determine the dress code. (After six o'clock in the evening is formal.)

Although some people are familiar with this point of etiquette, most are not. Therefore, you may wish to include "Black tie" on your reception cards to ensure that all of your guests know how to dress.

When using "Black tie," the *B* is uppercase and the *t* is lowercase. "Black tie" generally appears in the lower right-hand corner of the reception card. It does not appear on the invitation to the ceremony since it is the reception, not the ceremony, that is formal. When no reception card is used, "Black tie" appears in the lower right-hand corner of the invitation. If you do not like corner lines on invitations, you may include a reception card to indicate the type of dress.

What does "White tie" signify?

White-tie events are even more formal than black-tie events. They require men to wear white tie, wing collar, and tailcoat. Women wear evening gowns.

What does "R.s.v.p." stand for?

"R.s.v.p." is French for "Répondez s'il vous plaît." Its use on an invitation requires a response.

My reception is being held at my parents' house. How are my reception cards worded?

If your parents are hosting your wedding and their names are on the first line of the wedding invitations, the location lines on the reception cards show their home address. Your guests will know that it is their address because no other names are mentioned. When reply cards are not sent, the corner line on the reception card reads "The favour of a reply is requested," "R.s.v.p," or "R.S.V.P." Your parents' address is not shown beneath the reply request since it has already been given in the body of the reception card.

My reception is being held at a friend's house. How is that worded?

When a reception is held at the home of a friend, your friend's name and address are given on the location lines. A line reading, "at the residence of" precedes his or her name and address.

Reception
immediately following the ceremony
at the residence of
Mr. and Mrs. Michael Anthony LaPointe
211 Old Orchard Road
Bedford

My fiancé and I are saving our money to buy a house. Therefore, we would rather receive cash than gifts. How do we let our guests know this?

While an occasional bride and groom establish a money tree and ask their guests to contribute toward it, it is still considered incorrect and in very poor taste to ask your guests for money. First of all, it is presumptuous on your part to expect a gift from everybody to whom invitations are sent. Second, a number of your guests will probably want to give you a special gift to be remembered by. Asking for money directly is much too mercenary. (Of course, there is no reason why your parents, when asked, could not suggest a check.)

We have more household items than we could ever possibly use. How can we let our guests know that it is not necessary to give us any gifts?

Generally considered acceptable only when done by an older couple, a line reading, "No gifts, please" may be placed in the lower right-hand corner of your reception cards. A much nicer way of doing it, however, is to enclose a separate card with your invitations that reads, "Your presence is the only gift we request."

Our wedding is being held in a church and our reception will be at my parents' country club. Where on our wedding invitations does the reception information appear?

Weddings and receptions held at separate locations are considered separate events and require separate invitations. Reception cards serve as invitations to the reception and are used whenever the wedding and the reception are held in different locations. In the case of a formal wedding, it is not proper to put the reception information on the wedding invitation itself.

If you were doing a less formal wedding invitation and wanted to combine the wedding and reception information on one invitation, you could add a couple of lines to the invitation beneath the city and state that read, "and afterwards at the reception / Sleepy Hollow Country Club," "and afterward at the reception / Sleepy Hollow Country Club / Scarborough," or "Reception to follow / Sleepy Hollow Country Club / Scarborough."

Is it proper to have guests respond by phone or fax?

Formal social invitations are always responded to in writing. The use of a telephone or fax machine for responses is reserved for business and informal social occasions.

How do I let my guests know where I am registered?

It is in very poor taste to include a card announcing the store at which you are registered. That is too much like asking for a gift. The best way to let people know is by word of mouth.

We are having a formal wedding reception. I know that some of my friends do not own tuxedoes and I want them to feel comfortable attending in a suit. Is it proper to use "Black tie optional"?

The type of dress is never properly mentioned. The formality of dress is indicated by the time of day. (After six o'clock is considered formal.) "Black tie optional" is not correct and may cause confusion since it literally means that you may dress any way you please, with a tuxedo being one of the acceptable choices.

My reception is going to take place on a yacht. How is that worded?

The wording is similar to the wording on a standard reception card. The location line reads, "aboard the *Mirabella*" or whatever the name of the yacht is. The line beneath it shows the name of the yacht club or marina out of which it will sail.

How can we make sure that our guests don't miss the boat?

You may add two lines to the lower right-hand corner of your reception cards that read, "The *Mirabella* / sails promptly at eight o'clock."

REPLY CARDS AND ENVELOPES

Historically, women were the social secretaries of their households. Any correspondence that needed to be sent on behalf of the household was handled by the "lady of the house." Since she did not work outside the home (or inside, for that matter, since the "help" performed most of the household tasks), she had plenty of time to serve as social secretary. Among the functions she performed as social secretary was handwriting responses to invitations. Years ago, all responses to formal wedding invitations were handwritten on plain, unembellished letter sheets.

Over the past generations, women's roles have changed dramatically. As more and more women enter the labor force, the time they are able to devote to being social secretaries has decreased. That, and the fact that fewer and fewer people are now taught how to correctly respond to wedding invitations, leaves today's hosts in a quandary. While many would like to issue wedding invitations without reply cards, they are not sure that their guests will (or even know how to) respond. With the high costs involved in hosting a reception, hosts need to have as accurate a count as possible, so most are opting to use reply cards, which increases their chances of receiving replies. As the use of reply cards continues to grow, the custom of handwriting responses may disappear. (Despite the popularity of reply cards, however, many people still consider them improper and are insulted when they receive one, since they feel it suggests that they do not know how to respond properly.)

Reply cards can be engraved in a number of different formats. All formats, however, share similar features. Spaces are always provided for the guests' names and for their responses. A request for a response is always included as well, usually before a specific date. The reply request may be made in either the first two lines of the reply card or in the lower left-hand corner. Some brides choose not to include a date in their reply request as they feel it might insult guests who know very well when to reply. The name and address of whoever will receive the replies is engraved on the face of the reply envelopes. The copy may be centered or staggered.

M _____

will _____ *attend*

The favour of a reply is requested
before the ninth of August

_____

The favour of a reply

is requested before the ninth of August

M _____

will _____ *attend*

_____

M _____

_____ *will attend*

_____ *will not attend*

The favour of a reply
is requested before the ninth of August

Since my parents, my fiancé, and I are all doctors, many of our guests are also doctors. Should my reply cards be done differently?
Since many of your guests will be doctors, you may wish to omit the "M" on the reply cards. This leaves your reply cards with a blank name line and allows your guests to write in their appropriate titles.

I would like to receive handwritten responses but I'm afraid that if I don't send reply cards, I won't hear from everybody.
One solution is to send reply cards that are blank except for the words "The favour of a reply is requested" engraved across the top or bottom of the card. A second possibility is to take a small fold-over note, turn it on its side so that the fold is on the left-hand side, and engrave "The favour of a reply is requested" in the lower left-hand corner. This side-fold note becomes a miniature version of the letter sheet that is properly used for handwritten responses. It also seems to be a little more elegant than a card.

My family knows how to properly respond to wedding invitations but, unfortunately, my fiancé's family does not. Can I send reply cards to some guests and not to others?
If you are afraid of offending some of your guests by sending them reply cards, you may send reply cards just to those who you feel would need them. This, of course, requires two sets of reception cards: one with the reply request in the lower left-hand corner for those guests not receiving reply cards and another without the reply request for those guests who are receiving reply cards.

What date should be used for the reply request?
Most brides ask that their replies be received two weeks before their wedding date.

Our reception will feature a choice of three different meals. The caterer would like to know ahead of time how many of each to prepare. Is it proper to ask for that information on our reply cards?
It is not at all proper to include menu selections on reply cards. Most of the better restaurants and caterers are able to make an accurate enough estimate on their own. While some brides do run boxes for chicken, beef, and fish across the bottom of their reply cards, it is not in good taste.

Our caterer needs to know how many guests we expect at our wedding. Would it be helpful to put a line requesting "number of guests" on our reply cards?

Although having your guests fill in a space asking how many of them will be attending would definitely help you in obtaining an accurate count, there is one very serious drawback. By doing so, you encourage your guests to bring along more people than you otherwise would have invited. An invitation addressed to "Mr. and Mrs. Smith" with a reception card asking them how many people are coming might lead them to think that not only are they invited but also their kids and, perhaps, their Aunt Sally who, as it happens, will be in town that week. Giving your guests an opportunity like that can be asking for trouble.

AT-HOME CARDS

Family and friends can be made aware of your new address when at-home cards are included with your invitations and announcements. At-home cards are small enclosure cards whose card stock, lettering style, and ink color match the invitations with which they are sent. They alert people of the address at which you will be residing and the date after which you will be there. Although not done very often in the past, many couples now have their phone numbers engraved on their at-home cards.

The wording for at-home cards sent with announcements is different from the wording for at-home cards sent with invitations. At-home cards sent with announcements show your names together as "Mr. and Mrs." since you are already married when they are sent. When sent with invitations, your names are not used since you are not yet married and cannot use "Mr. and Mrs."

While the principal purpose of at-home cards is to let people know your new address, when sent with announcements they can also let people know that you have chosen to continue using your maiden name. Your name appears on the first line followed by your husband's name on line two. The remainder of the card reads as it normally would. Since you could have presented yourself as "Mrs." but did not, it will be assumed that you are still using your maiden name.

SENT WITH ANNOUNCEMENTS:

Mr. and Mrs. Nicholas Jude Strickland

after the tenth of September   *160 Central Park West • 12F*
                                        New York, New York 10023

SENT WITH INVITATIONS:

At home
after the tenth of September
160 Central Park West • 12F
New York, New York 10023
(212) 555-1212

I would like to send at-home cards with my wedding announcements but I don't want anybody to think that I'm asking for gifts.

At-home cards are like the change-of-address cards you might send when you move. They simply announce your new address and are a great convenience for anybody that wants to keep in touch with you. They are not gift-request cards and should never be interpreted as such.

What date should we use on our at-home cards?

Most couples use the date on which they return from their honeymoon.

DIRECTION AND MAP CARDS

Out-of-town guests will appreciate receiving direction cards or map cards. Direction cards give simple yet explicit directions to your wedding, while map cards are maps with the routes to your wedding highlighted. Map cards generally feature major roads and landmarks to help your guests find their way. When direction cards or map cards are used, the street address is not given on the invitations.

As with other enclosures, direction cards and map cards should complement the wedding invitations. They should be engraved in black ink on cards that match the invitations. To make them easier to read while driving, a sans serif (block) lettering style is usually used.

Direction cards and map cards are usually sent with the wedding invitations but may be sent afterwards in an envelope or as a postcard to those who accept your invitation. When sent afterwards, a line reading, "We are looking forward to having you attend" may be added to the top of the cards.

From New York City and Connecticut –

TAKE NEW YORK STATE THRUWAY (NORTH) TO EXIT 9. AT END OF EXIT RAMP, GO LEFT AT STOP SIGN. MAKE A LEFT AT THE NEXT LIGHT. MAKE A RIGHT AT THE FOLLOWING LIGHT TO THE TARRYTOWN HILTON.

From New Jersey –

TAKE NEW YORK STATE THRUWAY (SOUTH) TO EXIT 9. (FIRST EXIT AFTER TAPPAN ZEE TOLL). AT END OF RAMP CONTINUE STRAIGHT TO TARRYTOWN HILTON.

CEREMONY CARDS

For large receptions with small, private ceremonies, invitations are sent to the reception. Guests invited to the ceremony are sent smaller ceremony cards enclosed with their reception invitations. The same size as reception cards, ceremony cards serve as invitations to the ceremony. They are usually engraved to match the reception invitation but they may be handwritten when the guest list is small.

Despite the size of the card, a formal invitation format is used. "Request the honour of your presence" is used when the ceremony is held in a church while "request the pleasure of your company" is used when it is held elsewhere. Both "marriage ceremony" and "wedding ceremony" are proper. Whichever word ("marriage" or "wedding") is used on the reception invitations must be repeated on the ceremony cards.

The honour of your presence

is requested at the wedding ceremony

Saturday, the twenty-third of August

at six o'clock

Church of Christ

Bedford

ACCOMMODATION CARDS

Accommodation cards are enclosed with invitations sent to out-of-town guests who are unfamiliar with the area and need to make hotel reservations. They list the names and phone numbers of nearby hotels. If you are paying for your guests' rooms, a notation to that effect is made on the cards.

Accommodations
Westchester Marriott
(914) 555-1212
Inn on the Lake
(914) 555-1212

A room will be provided for you at:
Westchester Marriott
671 White Plains Road
Tarrytown, New York
(914) 555-1212

Please make reservations
before the sixteenth of August

WITHIN-THE-RIBBON CARDS

Pews may be cordoned off with white ribbons or cords to indicate a special seating section. When this is done, small cards reading "Within the ribbon" are sent with the invitations to those guests who will be seated in that section. The guests then bring the cards to the ceremony, which enables the ushers to seat them in the appropriate section.

PEW CARDS

Pew cards are used when specific pews have been assigned for some or all of the guests. This helps the ushers efficiently guide their guests to their assigned seats. Pew cards are sent with the invitations. A space on the card is filled in by hand with the appropriate pew.

Please present this card at

Church of Christ

Saturday, the twenty-third of August

Pew number ___3___

ADMISSION CARDS

Admission cards are a lot like tickets to the theater or to a ball game—you need to present them to gain admittance. Admission cards are generally used by well-known people who want to make sure that only invited guests are allowed to attend their wedding. They are sent with the invitations to all guests and may be personalized.

Mr. and Mrs. Glenn Rougeau

will please present this card at

Church of Christ

Saturday, the twenty-third of August

Please present this card at

Church of Christ

Saturday, the twenty-third of August

TRANSPORTATION CARDS

When a large number of out-of-town guests are attending a wedding, especially one in a big city, transportation from the wedding to the reception is occasionally provided. Sent with the invitations, transportation cards let your guests know that their local travel plans have been taken care of. The cards generally read, "Transportation will be provided / from the ceremony to the reception."

AT THE RECEPTION

Many times, it is the little things that make a reception special. While the meal, the dancing, and the company are the most obvious contributors to a successful reception, menu cards, place cards, table cards, and escort cards can also add elegance to your affair.

Escort cards are small cards that tell a gentleman which lady he is expected to escort into the reception. The gentleman's name is written on the envelope and the lady's name is written on the enclosed card.

Table cards and envelopes are efficient tools for directing your guests to their appointed seats. Placed in the entryway to the reception hall, the envelopes have your guests' names written on them. Inside the envelope, the card has the appropriate table number written on it. When it is time to be seated, your guests open the envelope with their names on it and head to the table indicated on the card.

When they arrive at their tables, your guests will notice place cards at each place setting. The place cards have just your guests' title and last name written on them. However, in situations where there is more than one "Mrs. Smith" seated at the table, first names are added.

Place cards are small white or ecru cards that may be trimmed in gold, silver, or in a decorative pattern. A small monogram—either the hosts' or the couple's—may be engraved at the top of the place cards.

Your guests may also find menu cards at their place settings. As the name suggests, menu cards list the menu items being served. The menu is listed in the center of the card. If wine is being served, the wines are listed alongside their appropriate courses. As with place cards, a monogram may be engraved at the top of the cards. Menu cards are usually shared by two people but there is no reason not to have one for each guest.

Menu cards are white or ecru cards that are usually trimmed in gold or silver that must match the place cards. For small receptions, they may be handwritten. For larger receptions, they should be engraved.

THANK-YOU NOTES

Thank-you notes give you the opportunity to express your appreciation to those who were kind enough to send wedding presents. In addition to conveying your appreciation, thank-you notes also let the recipients know that the gifts they sent were received and not lost in transit. They should be sent as soon after the wedding as possible. Your thank-you note will seem more sincere if it is sent in a timely manner.

Wedding thank-you notes are ecru or white foldover notes that match your wedding invitations. Your monogram is usually blind embossed or engraved in a conservative color on the front of the note.

Is it appropriate for me to send thank-you notes before my wedding?

You certainly may send thank-you notes before your wedding. Sending them as you receive the gifts is not only a courtesy to the people who sent them, it also cuts down the number you will need to send afterwards. However, remember at that point you still need to use stationery engraved with your maiden-name monogram.

How should my monogram read?

The thank-you notes that you send after your wedding have the initials of your first name, maiden name, and married name on them. If all of the initials in the monogram are the same size, your initials appear in order (first, maiden, married). When the monogram has a larger center initial, the center initial represents your married name. The initial on its left represents your first name while the initial on its right represents your maiden name (first, MARRIED, maiden).

Thank-you notes sent before the wedding should have your maiden-name monogram engraved on them. Your first name, middle name, and maiden name appear in that order in monograms in which all of the letters are the same size. In monograms with a larger center initial, the center initial represents your last name. It is flanked on the left by the initial representing your first name and on the right by the initial representing your middle name.

On what page do I start writing my thank-you notes?

Monograms appear in the mid-center of the first page of most wedding thank-you notes. When that is the case, you begin and end your note on page three. On some thank-you notes, the monogram may appear at the

top of the front page. If your monogram is at the top, you have the option of starting on either page one or page three. Your message should end on page three. (The whole point of using a small note is to limit the amount of verbiage you have to write.) If you do, however, have more to write, you would continue your message on page two. You should never write on the back of the note.

My husband-to-be will be writing some of our thank-you notes. How should our monogram read?

Thank-you notes, like any other social correspondence, are personal messages written by one person. The thank-you notes that you write may be written on behalf of you and your husband but they are still written by you and you alone. Therefore, only your monogram appears on them. Likewise, you sign just your name at the end of your note.

If your husband-to-be will be writing his share of thank-you notes, he does so on his own stationery. Men use correspondence cards instead of fold-over notes. Correspondence cards are flat cards that are mailed in their own envelopes. Your fiancé's name or monogram appears at the top of the card. He should only write on the front of his correspondence card, a rule he will come to appreciate after writing his first couple of thank-you notes.

The separate stationery that you and your husband-to-be use for your wedding thank-you notes can be used afterwards for any other short correspondences.

I am keeping my maiden name. My husband-to-be will be writing some of the thank-you notes. How should our monogram read?

Unfortunately, there has not yet been a monogram designed to handle your situation. Your best bet is to use two small, separate, matching monograms—yours on the left, his on the right—joined by a small diamond.

Of course, the more appropriate thing to do is for each of you to use your own stationery.

I am getting married for the second time. What initials do I use on my thank-you notes?

Second-time brides use the initials representing their first name, maiden name, and new married name. The initial representing their first married name is not used.

I am getting married for the third time. What initials do I use?
Third-time brides use the initials representing their first name, maiden name, and new married name. The initials representing their first and second married names are not used.

I am keeping my maiden name. What initials do I use?
Since your name is not changing, your monogram stays the same. You continue to use the initials of your first, middle, and last names.

Is it proper for me to use my middle name instead of my maiden name?
While some women continue to use their middle names after they are married, it is customary for them to use their maiden name as a middle name instead. By using their maiden names, married women can retain their identities as members of the families into which they were born.

I am hyphenating my maiden and married names. How does my monogram read?
The initials you use represent your first name, middle name, and hyphenated maiden and married names. All four of your initials appear in order in monograms in which all of the initials are the same size. Your hyphenated maiden and married names appear in the center of monograms that normally have a larger middle initial. The initial representing your first name appears to the left while your middle initial appears to the right. The hyphen does appear between your maiden and married initials. Since most monogram styles were designed for three initials, you should make sure that the monogram you choose looks good with four initials. Before ordering hundreds of notes, it might be a good idea to ask to see a proof.

My new last name is "McHenry." What initial do I use in my monogram?
You may use either *M* or *McH*. It is a matter of personal preference.

I would like to use single-initial notes for my prewedding thank-yous. Should I use my first or last initial?
Although there is no set rule, most women use the initial representing their last name on single-initial notes.

Is it proper to have our return address engraved on the envelope flaps?
Years ago, it was not considered proper for the return address to be engraved on the flaps on the envelopes in which wedding thank-you notes were sent. The return address was either handwritten or left off entirely. Today, the postal service requests that all mail carry a return address so it is now appropriate to have the return address engraved. It is also a great convenience.

How many thank-you notes should I order?
After you finish writing your thank-you notes, you may use your wedding notepaper for any short correspondence. Therefore, you should order enough to cover all your thank-yous plus extras for later on. It is a good idea to think ahead since stationery is less expensive per piece when ordered in larger quantities.

INFORMALS

Informals are small, fold-over notes that have a woman's full social name centered on the front. They are always ecru or white and are always engraved in black ink. To deviate from this format is to create something other than an informal. Informals were originally used for invitations to informal events, responses to informal events, reminders, and gift enclosure cards but not as thank-you notes. Nowadays, however, some brides also use informals for wedding thank-you notes.

When used as wedding thank-you notes, informals read, "Mrs." followed by the name of the groom. Since the informals will be used by the bride only, "Mr. and Mrs." should not appear on them. Informals that have "Mr. and Mrs." on them are appropriate only for informal invitations issued by both husband and wife.

Can the engraving plate I use for my "Mrs." informals also be used for "Mr. and Mrs." informals?
Yes, since in most cases the "Mr. and" can be omitted. In fact, it is a good idea when ordering "Mrs." informals to order an engraving plate with "Mr. and Mrs." for future use.

I am keeping my maiden name. How should my informals read?

Despite their name, informals are rather formal notes. Therefore, they normally require the use of a title. Unfortunately, there is no appropriate title for a married woman who uses her maiden name. "Miss" is not appropriate because it indicates that you are not and never have been married, "Mrs." is only correctly used with your husband's name, and "Ms." is not considered acceptable on social stationery. Your only option, therefore, is to use your maiden name without a title.

I am keeping my maiden name and my fiancé will be writing some of our thank-you notes. How should our informals read?

Although wedding thank-you notes are written on behalf of two people, only one person actually writes the note. Therefore, only one person's name properly appears on informals. If your fiancé will be writing some of the thank-you notes, he should do so on his own stationery.

Is it proper for us to use our first names on informals?

Since informals are actually formal notes, the use of first names on them would create "informal" informals. If you would like to use first names on your notepaper, you should use less formal stationery such as a colorful note or correspondence card.

WRITING THANK-YOU NOTES

Finding a personal note or letter waiting for us at the end of the day is always a pleasant surprise. Letters from friends and loved ones are special gifts. Somebody has taken time from their busy schedule to share their personal thoughts with you. And, because of the permanence of a letter, it can be enjoyed over and over again.

If a letter is such a special gift, why do we write so few of them? In an age in which it is so convenient to pick up the telephone, we see letter writing as a major event. We think that every letter or note must be a masterpiece.

Writing becomes a task because we feel that the quality of our letters must transcend the ordinary. Yet, when we receive a letter, we appreciate what was written and the thought that went into it, not how well it was written.

There are a few simple hints to follow to help you write your thank-you notes. Most of them simply require you to be yourself. Remember, the people to whom you are writing want to hear from you. They want to hear that you received their gifts and that you appreciate them immensely.

DON'T WORRY ABOUT STYLE

Write your thank-you notes in the style in which you usually speak. Use contractions; they're more personal. They'll make your notes sound more like you.

DON'T LET YOUR THANK-YOU OBLIGATIONS PILE UP

Write your thank-you notes the day you receive your presents. Your notes will be fresher and will sound more sincere.

JUST WRITE

Writer's block comes from thinking too much about style and substance. You know pretty much what you want to say. Just say it. And don't worry about repeating yourself. Everybody understands that it's impossible to write something original on each and every thank-you note. Besides, your thank-you notes are not going to be passed around and compared.

Thank-you notes should be sent to everybody who sent you a gift or helped you with your wedding. If you ever wonder whether or not a situation calls for a thank-you note, stop wondering and send one. Whether necessary or not, it is always welcome.

Your thank-you notes should be handwritten and they may be brief. Since you write the thank-you notes yourself, you sign the notes with just your name. You may sign just your first name when writing to those closest to you and your first, maiden, and married names when writing to those who may need all three names to recognize you.

A tasteful thank-you note contains four basic parts:

1. A GREETING:
   Dear Aunt Kelly and Uncle Steven,

2. A NOTE OF THANKS:
   The antique candlesticks that you gave us are beautiful. We really appreciate all the love that went into choosing them.

3. A MENTION OF HOW USEFUL THEIR GIFT WILL BE:
   A place of honor has been reserved for them on our dining room table.

4. A SUGGESTION TO SEE THEM SOON:
   Nicholas and I plan on inviting you for dinner—and to admire our new candlesticks—as soon as we get settled in.

Love,
Jennifer

GIFT-ACKNOWLEDGMENT CARDS

Back in the days when a honeymoon meant, for some, a cruise around the world or a summer in Europe, gift-acknowledgment cards were used to postpone the bride's obligation to send personal thank-you notes. Today, however, the reason is more likely an extraordinary number of gifts or pressing professional responsibilities. Nevertheless, gift-acknowledgment cards are still sent—sometimes even by the bride's mother—to buy the bride and groom additional time to send their thank-you notes.

Gift-acknowledgment cards do not take the place of thank-you notes. They merely acknowledge the fact that a gift has been received and mention that a personal thank-you note is forthcoming.

Mrs. Nicholas Jude Strickland

has received your very kind gift

and will write you later of her appreciation

CALLING CARDS

Calling cards made their first appearance during the late 1600s. They were small, decorative cards with hand-painted borders. Engraved in the center of the cards were the individuals' names and hereditary titles. Through the years, their appearance changed. The decorative borders gradually went out of style. By the 1800s, the borders disappeared completely and calling cards began to take on the look that they have today.

Early calling cards were left by the European aristocracy when paying calls on fellow aristocrats. This practice eventually spread around the world. In the United States, it evolved into a very formal ritual with very stringent rules. Upper-crust women reserved one day a week to stay at home and receive calls. Other society ladies, knowing which day to call, stopped by and handed the butler their cards. After perusing the card, Madame decided whether or not she was receiving at that time. If she chose to receive your call, you were led into her drawing room where you chatted for a short period of time. You never stayed too long since she had other callers to receive. If she chose not to see you, you left your card and went on to your next call. This was easily done since, in most towns, calling days were set up by neighborhood. It could be uptown on Mondays, downtown on Tuesdays, and midtown on Wednesdays. Thursdays might be set aside for the east side with Fridays reserved for the west side.

There were also rules concerning how many cards to leave and to whom they might be left. A woman could leave but one card as she was only permitted to call on another woman. A man, on the other hand, could leave up to three cards; one for the man of the house, one for the lady, and one for the couple. Turning down one of the corners of the card signified that it was intended for all the ladies of the house.

Although still practiced in military and diplomatic circles, "calling" is no longer practiced by the general population. However, calling cards still exist and are used for such diverse purposes as gift enclosures, informal invitations (although they are too small to mail), and to hand out to people one might meet in social situations, much as one would a business card in a business setting. Indeed, the calling card was the forerunner of the modern business card.

Calling cards are always engraved in black ink on small, white or ecru cards. The cards come in a variety of sizes. Each size designates its owner's sex and marital status. The correct sizes are listed below:

Children twelve and younger	2¼ by 1⅜ inches
Single women	2⅞ by 2 inches
Married women	3⅛ by 2¼ inches
Men	3⅜ by 1½ inches or
	3½ by 2 inches
Married couple	3⅜ by 2½ inches

The etiquette for calling cards is the same as the etiquette used for weddings. Since calling cards are formal social cards, names and social titles are used. Men and women under the age of eighteen, however, do not use titles. Some older women, especially those who are divorced, choose not to use their titles either.

Calling cards should be ordered with envelopes if they are going to be used as gift enclosures.

Is it proper to use "Ms." on calling cards?

Since calling cards are formal, "Ms." is not used. Women may, however, drop their titles altogether.

Is it proper to use abbreviations?

All titles except "Mr." and "Mrs." should be written out. Some titles, however, may be abbreviated when space is a problem. "The Reverend," however, is never abbreviated. If additional space is needed, the middle name may be omitted.

Is it proper to use initials?

Initials are not properly used on calling cards. All names should be written out.

Is it proper to put addresses on calling cards?

While it is proper to have your address engraved in the lower right-hand corner, it is more personal to add it in your own handwriting. This honors the recipient since it suggests that you do not give your address out to just anybody.

FORMAL RESPONSES

Although most wedding invitations are sent with reply cards, many are sent with a reply request engraved on the reception card instead. These invitations require a handwritten response. Formal responses are handwritten on ecru or white letter sheets. These sheets were traditionally blank but may now have a tasteful monogram blind embossed at the top.

Responses follow the format of the invitations. Since wedding invitations are issued in the third person, responses are written in the third person as well. The guests' full social names and titles are used while only the hosts' titles and surnames are written. On the envelopes, however, the hosts' full names are used with their titles. Acceptances repeat the date and time of the wedding while regrets repeat just the date. There is no need to mention the reason for not attending.

Acceptance:

Mr. and Mrs. Edward Allen Singer
accept with pleasure
the kind invitation of
Mr. and Mrs. Forrester
for Saturday, the twenty-third of August
at six o'clock

Regret:

Mr. and Mrs. Edward Allen Singer
regret that they are unable to accept
the kind invitation of
Mr. and Mrs. Forrester
for Saturday, the twenty-third of August

In what color ink should responses be written?

Formal responses may be written in blue or black ink. Most people, however, prefer black ink since it usually matches the invitations.

When should responses be sent?

Most invitations mention the date before which the responses are needed. Your response should be mailed so that it arrives before its deadline. If no date is mentioned, responses should be sent three days after the invitation is received.

How is the response written when children are invited?

The names used in your response should be the same as those written on the inside envelope of the invitation you received. If your children are invited, their names will be listed on the face of the inside envelope, beneath yours. When writing your response, repeat the names as they are written on the inside envelope.

Mr. and Mrs. Edward Allen Singer
Esta, Janice and Barbara
accept with pleasure
etc.

My husband and I were both invited to my cousin's wedding. I will be able to go but my husband will be out of town. How should my response read?

Your response begins with a formal acceptance on your part. Your husband's regret is added at the end.

Mrs. Edward Allen Singer
accepts with pleasure
the kind invitation of
Mr. and Mrs. Forrester
for Saturday, the twenty-third of August
at six o'clock
Mr. Edward Allen Singer
regrets that he is unable to attend

FILLING IN REPLY CARDS

Reply cards are easier to use than they appear to be. A space, usually following an "M," is provided for your titles and names. (The "M" is provided to help you get started with your title, assuming your title begins with an "M." If it does not, you may draw a slash through the "M" and write out "Doctor" or whatever your title may be.) The next line allows you to tell your hosts whether or not you will be attending. If you are, the space is left blank. If you are unable to attend, you write in, "not." You then place the card inside its envelope and mail it.

ACCEPTANCE:

The favour of a reply

is requested before the ninth of August

M̶ r. and Mrs. Glenn Rougeau

will _____ attend

REGRET:

The favour of a reply

is requested before the ninth of August

M̲ r̲ a̲n̲d̲ M̲r̲s̲.̲ G̲l̲e̲n̲n̲ R̲o̲u̲g̲e̲a̲u̲

will ̲n̲o̲t̲ *attend*

What names are used on reply cards?
Your full social names with titles are used. If you are married, your names read, "Mr. and Mrs." followed by your husband's first, middle, and last names.

I received a blank reply card with just "The favour of a reply" on it. What should I do?
Blank reply cards are sent when a bride would like a formal response but is afraid that if she does not send reply cards, she will not get many responses. Since the bride provided you the card and the opportunity to write a formal response, you should do so.

My granddaughter's wedding invitations arrived with reply cards enclosed. I detest those things and would rather send a proper reply. Would that be proper?
It is always proper to send a formal response to a formal invitation.

APPENDIX

FORMS OF ADDRESS FOR
DIPLOMATIC LEADERS *

* The following copy should be one line whenever possible, but may be split, as shown, when two lines would be more aesthetically pleasing.

THE PRESIDENT OF THE UNITED STATES

Man

INVITATION

The President and Mrs. Robinson

OUTSIDE ENVELOPE   INSIDE ENVELOPE

The President and Mrs. Robinson   The President and Mrs. Robinson

Woman

INVITATION

The President and Mr. Robinson

OUTSIDE ENVELOPE   INSIDE ENVELOPE

The President and Mr. Robinson   The President and Mr. Robinson

FORMER PRESIDENT OF THE UNITED STATES

Man

INVITATION

Mr. and Mrs. William Robinson

OUTSIDE ENVELOPE   INSIDE ENVELOPE

The Honorable William Robinson   Mr. and Mrs. Robinson
and Mrs. Robinson

Woman

INVITATION

Mr. and Mrs. William Robinson

OUTSIDE ENVELOPE   INSIDE ENVELOPE

The Honorable Lesley Robinson   Mr. and Mrs. Robinson
and Mr. Robinson

THE VICE PRESIDENT OF THE UNITED STATES

Man

INVITATION

The Vice President and Mrs. Robinson

OUTSIDE ENVELOPE
The Vice President
and Mrs. Robinson

INSIDE ENVELOPE
The Vice President
and Mrs. Robinson

Woman

INVITATION

The Vice President and Mr. Robinson

OUTSIDE ENVELOPE
The Vice President and
Mr. Robinson

INSIDE ENVELOPE
The Vice President and
Mr. Robinson

MEMBER OF THE CABINET

Man

INVITATION

The Secretary of State and Mrs. Robinson

OUTSIDE ENVELOPE
The Secretary of State
and Mrs. Robinson

INSIDE ENVELOPE
The Secretary of State
and Mrs. Robinson

Woman

INVITATION

The Secretary of State and Mr. Robinson

OUTSIDE ENVELOPE
The Secretary of State
and Mr. Robinson

INSIDE ENVELOPE
The Secretary of State
and Mr. Robinson

United States Senator

Man

INVITATION

Mr. and Mrs. William Robinson

or

Senator and Mrs. William Robinson

OUTSIDE ENVELOPE

INSIDE ENVELOPE

The Honorable William Robinson and Mrs. Robinson

Senator and Mrs. Robinson

Woman

INVITATION

Mr. and Mrs. William Robinson

or

Senator Lesley Robinson
and Mr. William Robinson

OUTSIDE ENVELOPE

INSIDE ENVELOPE

The Honorable Lesley Robinson
and Mr. Robinson

Mr. and Mrs. Robinson

or

or

The Honorable Lesley Robinson
and Mr. Robinson

Senator Robinson
and Mr. Robinson

The Speaker of the House

Man

INVITATION

The Speaker of the House and Mrs. Robinson

or

The Speaker and Mrs. Robinson

OUTSIDE ENVELOPE

INSIDE ENVELOPE

The Speaker of the House
and Mrs. Robinson

The Speaker of the House
and Mrs. Robinson

or

or

The Speaker and Mrs. Robinson

The Speaker and Mrs. Robinson

Woman

INVITATION
The Speaker of the House and Mr. Robinson
or
The Speaker and Mr. Robinson

OUTSIDE ENVELOPE
The Speaker of the House
and Mr. Robinson
or
The Speaker and Mr. Robinson

INSIDE ENVELOPE
The Speaker of the House
and Mr. Robinson
or
The Speaker and Mr. Robinson

MEMBER OF THE HOUSE OF REPRESENTATIVES

Man

INVITATION
Mr. and Mrs. William Robinson

OUTSIDE ENVELOPE
The Honorable William Robinson
and Mrs. Robinson

INSIDE ENVELOPE
Mr.and Mrs. Robinson

Woman

INVITATION
Mr. and Mrs. William Robinson

OUTSIDE ENVELOPE
The Honorable Lesley Robinson
and Mr. Robinson

INSIDE ENVELOPE
Mr. and Mrs. Robinson

THE CHIEF JUSTICE OF THE SUPREME COURT

Man

INVITATION
The Chief Justice and Mrs. Robinson

OUTSIDE ENVELOPE
The Chief Justice
and Mrs. Robinson

INSIDE ENVELOPE
The Chief Justice
and Mrs. Robinson

Woman
INVITATION

The Chief Justice and Mr. Robinson

OUTSIDE ENVELOPE
The Chief Justice
and Mr. Robinson

INSIDE ENVELOPE
The Chief Justice
and Mr. Robinson

ASSOCIATE JUSTICE OF THE SUPREME COURT

Man
INVITATION

Mr. Justice Robinson and Mrs. Robinson

OUTSIDE ENVELOPE
Mr. Justice Robinson and
Mrs. Robinson

INSIDE ENVELOPE
Justice and Mrs. Robinson

Woman
INVITATION

Madam Justice Robinson and Mr. Robinson

OUTSIDE ENVELOPE
Madam Justice Robinson and
Mr. Robinson

INSIDE ENVELOPE
Justice Robinson
and Mr. Robinson

UNITED STATES AMBASSADOR TO THE UNITED NATIONS

Man
INVITATION

Mr. and Mrs. William Robinson

OUTSIDE ENVELOPE
The United States Representative
to the United Nations
and Mrs. Robinson

INSIDE ENVELOPE
The United States Representative
to the United Nations
and Mrs. Robinson

Woman

INVITATION

Mr. and Mrs. William Robinson

OUTSIDE ENVELOPE	INSIDE ENVELOPE
The United States Representative	The United States Representative
to the United Nations	to the United Nations
and Mr. Robinson	and Mr. Robinson

A M E R I C A N   A M B A S S A D O R   (A T   P O S T)

Man

INVITATION

The American Ambassador and Mrs. Robinson

or

Mr. and Mrs. William Robinson

OUTSIDE ENVELOPE	INSIDE ENVELOPE
The Honorable	The Honorable
The American Ambassador	The American Ambassador
and Mrs. Robinson	and Mrs. Robinson

Woman

INVITATION

The American Ambassador and Mr. Robinson

or

Mr. and Mrs. William Robinson

OUTSIDE ENVELOPE	INSIDE ENVELOPE
The Honorable	The Honorable
The American Ambassador	The American Ambassador
and Mr. Robinson	and Mr. Robinson

AMERICAN AMBASSADOR TO LATIN AMERICAN COUNTRIES (AT POST)

Man

INVITATION

The Ambassador of the United States of America
and Mrs. Robinson

or

Mr. and Mrs. William Robinson

OUTSIDE ENVELOPE	INSIDE ENVELOPE
The Honorable	The Honorable
The Ambassador of the	The Ambassador of the
United States	United States
and Mrs. Robinson	and Mrs. Robinson

Woman

INVITATION

The Ambassador of the United States of America
and Mr. Robinson

or

Mr. and Mrs. William Robinson

OUTSIDE ENVELOPE	INSIDE ENVELOPE
The Honorable	The Honorable
The Ambassador of the	The Ambassador of the
United States	United States
and Mr. Robinson	and Mr. Robinson

AMERICAN AMBASSADOR (AWAY FROM POST)

Man

INVITATION

The American Ambassador to Switzerland
and Mrs. Robinson

or

The American Ambassador and Mrs. Robinson

or

Mr. and Mrs. William Robinson

OUTSIDE ENVELOPE

The Honorable
The American Ambassador
to Switzerland
and Mrs. Robinson

INSIDE ENVELOPE

The Honorable
The American Ambassador
to Switzerland
and Mrs. Robinson

Woman

INVITATION

The American Ambassador to Switzerland
and Mr. Robinson

or

The American Ambassador and Mr. Robinson

or

Mr. and Mrs. William Robinson

OUTSIDE ENVELOPE

The Honorable
The American Ambassador
to Switzerland
and Mr. Robinson

INSIDE ENVELOPE

The Honorable
The American Ambassador
to Switzerland
and Mr. Robinson

AMERICAN AMBASSADOR TO LATIN AMERICAN COUNTRIES (AWAY FROM POST)

Man

INVITATION

The Ambassador of the United States of America to Chile
and Mrs. Robinson

or

Mr. and Mrs. William Robinson

OUTSIDE ENVELOPE

The Honorable
The Ambassador of the United
States to Chile
and Mrs. Robinson

INSIDE ENVELOPE

The Honorable
The Ambassador of the United
States to Chile
and Mrs. Robinson

Woman
INVITATION

The Ambassador of the United States of America to Chile
and Mr. Robinson

or

Mr. and Mrs. William Robinson

OUTSIDE ENVELOPE	INSIDE ENVELOPE
The Honorable	The Honorable
The Ambassador of the United	The Ambassador of the United
States to Chile	States to Chile
and Mr. Robinson	and Mr. Robinson

GOVERNOR

Man
INVITATION

The Governor of Massachusetts and Mrs. Robinson

OUTSIDE ENVELOPE	INSIDE ENVELOPE
The Governor and Mrs. Robinson	The Governor and Mrs. Robinson

Woman
INVITATION

The Governor of Massachusetts and Mr. Robinson

OUTSIDE ENVELOPE	INSIDE ENVELOPE
The Governor and Mr. Robinson	The Governor and Mr. Robinson

STATE SENATOR OR REPRESENTATIVE

Man
INVITATION

Mr. and Mrs. William Robinson

OUTSIDE ENVELOPE	INSIDE ENVELOPE
The Honorable William Robinson	Mr. and Mrs. Robinson
and Mrs. Robinson	

Woman

INVITATION
Mr. and Mrs. William Robinson

OUTSIDE ENVELOPE	INSIDE ENVELOPE
The Honorable Lesley Robinson and Mr. Robinson	Mr. and Mrs. Robinson

M A Y O R

Man

INVITATION
The Mayor of Dalton and Mrs. Robinson

OUTSIDE ENVELOPE	INSIDE ENVELOPE
The Honorable William Robinson and Mrs. Robinson	Mr. and Mrs. Robinson

Woman

INVITATION
The Mayor of Dalton and Mr. Robinson

OUTSIDE ENVELOPE	INSIDE ENVELOPE
The Honorable Lesley Robinson and Mr. Robinson	Mr. and Mrs. Robinson

FORMS OF ADDRESS FOR RELIGIOUS LEADERS *

* The following copy should be one line whenever possible, but may be split, as shown, when two lines would be more aesthetically pleasing.

R O M A N   C A T H O L I C   C H U R C H

The Pope

INVITATION
His Holiness, the Pope

OUTSIDE ENVELOPE	INSIDE ENVELOPE
His Holiness, the Pope	His Holiness, the Pope
or	
His Holiness, Pope John Paul II	

Cardinal

INVITATION

Cardinal Robinson

OUTSIDE ENVELOPE

His Eminence, William Cardinal
Robinson

INSIDE ENVELOPE

Cardinal Robinson

Archbishop

INVITATION

Archbishop Robinson

OUTSIDE ENVELOPE

The Most Reverend William
Robinson

INSIDE ENVELOPE

Archbishop Robinson

Bishop

INVITATION

Bishop Robinson

OUTSIDE ENVELOPE

The Most Reverend William
Robinson

INSIDE ENVELOPE

Bishop Robinson

Abbot

INVITATION

Abbot Robinson

OUTSIDE ENVELOPE

The Right Reverend William
Robinson

INSIDE ENVELOPE

Abbot Robinson

Monsignor

INVITATION

Monsignor Robinson

OUTSIDE ENVELOPE

The Right Reverend Monsignor
William Robinson

INSIDE ENVELOPE

Monsignor Robinson

Priest

INVITATION
The Reverend William Robinson

OUTSIDE ENVELOPE	INSIDE ENVELOPE
The Reverend William Robinson	Father Robinson

Brother

INVITATION
Brother William Robinson

OUTSIDE ENVELOPE	INSIDE ENVELOPE
Brother William Robinson	Brother William

Mother Superior

INVITATION
Mother Lesley Robinson

OUTSIDE ENVELOPE	INSIDE ENVELOPE
Mother Lesley Robinson	Mother Robinson

Sister

INVITATION
Sister Lesley Robinson

OUTSIDE ENVELOPE	INSIDE ENVELOPE
Sister Lesley Robinson	Sister Robinson

EPISCOPAL CHURCH

Presiding Bishop

INVITATION
Bishop and Mrs. William Robinson

OUTSIDE ENVELOPE	INSIDE ENVELOPE
The Right Reverend and Mrs. William Robinson	The Right Reverend and Mrs. Robinson

Bishop/Man

INVITATION
Bishop and Mrs. William Robinson

OUTSIDE ENVELOPE	INSIDE ENVELOPE
The Right Reverend and Mrs. William Robinson	The Right Reverend and Mrs. Robinson

Bishop/Woman

INVITATION

Mr. and Mrs. William Robinson

or

Bishop Lesley Robinson
and Mr. William Robinson

OUTSIDE ENVELOPE

Mr. and Mrs. William Robinson

or

The Right Reverend Lesley
Robinson
and Mr. William Robinson

INSIDE ENVELOPE

Mr. and Mrs. Robinson

or

Bishop Robinson
and Mr. Robinson

Archdeacon/Man

INVITATION

Archdeacon and Mrs. William Robinson

OUTSIDE ENVELOPE

The Venerable and Mrs. William
Robinson

INSIDE ENVELOPE

The Venerable and Mrs. Robinson

Archdeacon/Woman

INVITATION

Mr. and Mrs. William Robinson

or

Archdeacon Lesley Robinson
and Mr. William Robinson

OUTSIDE ENVELOPE

Mr. and Mrs. William Robinson

or

The Venerable Lesley Robinson
and Mr. William Robinson

INSIDE ENVELOPE

Mr. and Mrs. Robinson

or

Archdeacon Robinson
and Mr. Robinson

Dean/Man

INVITATION

Dean and Mrs. William Robinson

OUTSIDE ENVELOPE

The Very Reverend
and Mrs. William Robinson

INSIDE ENVELOPE

The Very Reverend and
Mrs. Robinson

Dean/Woman

INVITATION

Mr. and Mrs. William Robinson

or

Dean Lesley Robinson
and Mr. William Robinson

OUTSIDE ENVELOPE
Mr. and Mrs. William Robinson
or
The Very Reverend Lesley
Robinson and Mr. William
Robinson

INSIDE ENVELOPE
Mr. and Mrs. Robinson
or
Dean Robinson
and Mr. Robinson

Canon/Man

INVITATION
Canon and Mrs. William Robinson

OUTSIDE ENVELOPE
The Reverend and Mrs. William
Robinson

INSIDE ENVELOPE
The Reverend and Mrs. Robinson

Canon/Woman

INVITATION
Mr. and Mrs. William Robinson
or
Canon Lesley Robinson
and Mr. William Robinson

OUTSIDE ENVELOPE
Mr. and Mrs. William Robinson
or
The Reverend Lesley Robinson
and Mr. William Robinson

INSIDE ENVELOPE
Mr. and Mrs. Robinson
or
Canon Robinson
and Mr. Robinson

PROTESTANT CHURCHES

Minister or Pastor/Man

INVITATION
The Reverend and Mrs. William Robinson

OUTSIDE ENVELOPE
The Reverend and Mrs. William
Robinson

INSIDE ENVELOPE
The Reverend and Mrs. Robinson

Minister or Pastor/Woman

INVITATION

Mr. and Mrs. William Robinson

or

The Reverend Lesley Robinson
and Mr. William Robinson

OUTSIDE ENVELOPE	INSIDE ENVELOPE
Mr. and Mrs. William Robinson	Mr. and Mrs. Robinson
or	or
The Reverend Lesley Robinson and Mr. William Robinson	Reverend Robinson and Mr. Robinson
	or
	Pastor Robinson and Mr. Robinson

Minister or Pastor with Doctorate/Man

INVITATION

The Reverend Doctor and Mrs. William Robinson

OUTSIDE ENVELOPE	INSIDE ENVELOPE
The Reverend Doctor and Mrs. William Robinson	The Reverend Doctor and Mrs. Robinson

Minister or Pastor with Doctorate/Woman

INVITATION

Mr. and Mrs. William Robinson

or

The Reverend Doctor Lesley Robinson
and Mr. William Robinson

OUTSIDE ENVELOPE	INSIDE ENVELOPE
Mr. and Mrs. William Robinson	Mr. and Mrs. Robinson
or	or
The Reverend Doctor Lesley Robinson and Mr. Robinson	The Reverend Doctor Robinson and Mr. Robinson

CHURCH OF JESUS CHRIST OF LATTER-DAY SAINTS

Mormon Bishop

INVITATION

Mr. and Mrs. William Robinson

OUTSIDE ENVELOPE	INSIDE ENVELOPE
Mr. and Mrs. William Robinson	Mr. and Mrs. William Robinson

JEWISH FAITH

Rabbi/Man

INVITATION

Rabbi and Mrs. Irving Horowitz

OUTSIDE ENVELOPE	INSIDE ENVELOPE
Rabbi and Mrs. Irving Horowitz	Rabbi and Mrs. Horowitz

Rabbi/Woman

INVITATION

Mr. and Mrs. Irving Horowitz

or

Rabbi Miriam Horowitz
and Mr. Irving Horowitz

OUTSIDE ENVELOPE	INSIDE ENVELOPE
Mr. and Mrs. Irving Horowitz	Mr. and Mrs. Horowitz
or	or
Rabbi Miriam Horowitz	Rabbi Horowitz
and Mr. Irving Horowitz	and Mr. Horowitz

Rabbi with Doctorate/Man

INVITATION

Rabbi and Mrs. Irving Horowitz

OUTSIDE ENVELOPE	INSIDE ENVELOPE
Rabbi and Mrs. Irving Horowitz	Rabbi and Mrs. Horowitz

Rabbi with Doctorate/Woman

INVITATION

Mr. and Mrs. Irving Horowitz

or

Rabbi Miriam Horowitz

and Mr. Irving Horowitz

OUTSIDE ENVELOPE	INSIDE ENVELOPE
Mr. and Mrs. Irving Horowitz	Mr. and Mrs. Horowitz
or	or
Rabbi Miriam Horowitz	Rabbi Horowitz
and Mr. Irving Horowitz	and Mr. Horowitz

Cantor/Man

INVITATION

Cantor and Mrs. Irving Horowitz

OUTSIDE ENVELOPE	INSIDE ENVELOPE
Cantor and Mrs. Irving Horowitz	Cantor and Mrs. Horowitz

Cantor/Woman

INVITATION

Mr. and Mrs. Irving Horowitz

or

Cantor Miriam Horowitz

and Mr. Irving Horowitz

OUTSIDE ENVELOPE	INSIDE ENVELOPE
Mr. and Mrs. Irving Horowitz	Mr. and Mrs. Horowitz
or	or
Cantor Miriam Horowitz	Cantor Horowitz
and Mr. Irving Horowitz	and Mr. Horowitz

For almost two hundred years, Crane and Co. has produced the finest papers in the world. Established in 1801 by Zenas Crane, Crane & Co. is still a family-owned, privately held company located in Dalton, Massachusetts. For generations, Crane's wedding invitations and social stationery has been available at only the finest stores. It has been used by presidents, kings and queens, and by everybody who appreciates stationery of the finest quality.

The company Zenas Crane founded has grown, prospered, and diversified, still makes paper from 100 percent cotton, and still adheres to the quality standards on which he insisted.

Crane products today include currency and security papers (including paper for United States currency since 1879), architectural and engineering drafting papers, specialized products for technical applications such as filtration and electrical insulation, and a full line of business and social stationery papers for corporate letterheads, social correspondence, and wedding invitations and announcements.

ABOUT THE AUTHOR

Steven L. Feinberg directs customer training and development for Crane & Co., Inc., and travels throughout the country teaching Crane customers the etiquette, uses, and benefits of fine stationery and invitations. He is the author of *Crane's Blue Book of Stationery* and lives in Dalton, Massachusetts.